America: To Pray Or Not To Pray?

A statistical look at what happened when religious principles were separated from public affairs

by

David Barton

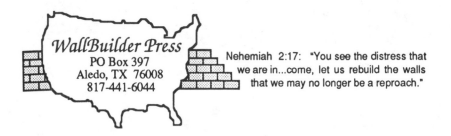

WallBuilder Press
PO Box 397
Aledo, TX 76008
817-441-6044

Nehemiah 2:17: "You see the distress that we are in...come, let us rebuild the walls that we may no longer be a reproach."

WallBuilder Press
P.O. Box 397
Aledo, Texas 76008
817-441-6044

Printed in the United States of America
ISBN 0-925279-16-1

Acknowledgments

This book was very much a "team" project, or in the words of the Apostle Paul, it was the accomplishment of numerous "fellow-workers." Several individuals made important contributions to this work and I want to acknowledge and thank them. First, thanks are due to the Lord God Who sparked within me the original idea of this statistical examination, Who provided direction during the entire project, and Who efficiently guided us to the proper sources to acquire the raw data. Second, thanks to my wife, Cheryl, a gift "from the Lord" (Proverbs 19:14), who cheerfully endured my 18-hour work days and continually encouraged me through this endeavor—indeed, she is a wife "worth far more than rubies" (Proverbs 31:10); and thanks to my parents, Grady and Rose, who instilled in me a love for hard-work, thoroughness, and persistence, without which this work never would have been possible.

Next, my thanks to several co-workers: Kit Marshall, who fastidiously pursued the collection of the data and who spent countless hours seeking "needles in haystacks"; Mike Ward, who managed to turn the raw data into readable charts and graphs; Bob Lewis, who became a middle-man in a modem "war," receiving and transmitting information to all corners of the nation at all hours of the day and night; Tom and Barbara Smiley, Knox and Kay Ross, and Grady and Rose Barton, who read the rough draft, edited it, re-read it, re-edited it, etc., etc., until reaching this final form. Indeed, the fact that this was a "team" project makes it a better product; as Proverbs 24:6 discloses, "For waging war you need guidance, and for victory *many advisers.*"

For these named individuals, and for the many other unnamed individuals who also contributed to this work, I offer the same sentiment expressed by the Apostle Paul in Philippians 1:3: "I thank my God every time I remember you." My sincere prayer to God for this finished product is that *"Your* kingdom come, *Your* will be done, on earth as it is in heaven" (Matthew 6:10).

David Barton
May 1991

America:
To Pray Or Not To Pray?

Table of Contents

Index to Charts, Tables, and Graphs

Preface

God's leading seemed so "non-spiritual" that I questioned it, but it was so strong that I could not ignore it. In July 1987, God impressed me to do two things. First, I was to search the library and find the date that prayer had been prohibited in public schools. Second, I was to obtain a record of national SAT scores (the academic test given to prospective college-bound high school students) spanning the last several decades. I didn't know why, but I somehow knew that these two pieces of information would be very important.

I had believed that the two instructions were separate and distinct, yet I soon discovered that they were unquestionably related. I first obtained the SAT scores. I noticed that while the scores had been relatively stable from 1952-1962, their decline had been so rapid after 1963 that it seemed as if they were tumbling down a steep mountainside. Next, I discovered that corporate verbal prayer first had been forbidden to public school students in a limited manner on June 25, 1962, and, in a second far-reaching decision on June 17, 1963, had been completely removed.

When I plotted the two items, I was astounded! I thought to myself, "Can it *really* be possible that prayer was removed in '62 and academics began to decline in '63?" But the correlation appeared clear. I felt I was now armed with some astonishing statistical information; I just didn't know what to do with it!

In the fall, I had opportunity to present the two pieces of information to a U.S. Congressman. He, too, was amazed at the apparent correlation. He informed us that, to his knowledge, in all the Congressional controversy surrounding the attempt to return religious principles to schools, statistical information had never been presented to Congress. School prayer had always previously been a "religious" issue only— this was the first time in his extended tenure in Congress that he had seen information suggesting any tangible effect of religious principles in schools. He stared at the chart, shook his head, and declared, "Someone ought to research this!"

SAT Total Scores

Although the Congressman had voiced the words, the effect was the same as if God Himself had personally delivered a commission to me.

After returning home, God outlined the strategy for pursuing further research through a comment made by our secretary. She was examining the simple 22-word prayer from the *Engel v. Vitale* case (the 1962 case the Court used to negate all school prayer):

Almighty God, we acknowledge our dependence upon Thee, and we beg Thy blessings upon us, our parents, our teachers and our Country.

As we were discussing how the removal of such a simple prayer might have so profoundly affected the SAT scores, she observed that all four of the areas mentioned in the students' prayer (students, families, schools, and the nation) probably had declined dramatically since 1962. Even though she voiced the words, the effect on me was the same as it had been at the Congressman's office—it was as if God again clearly had spoken.

My curiosity was stirred. Had the change in national policy—the separation of religious principles from public affairs—resulted in any measurable difference for young people, their families, their schools, and their nation? I somehow knew that statistics would be available and that undoubtedly they would demonstrate that the inclusion of religious principles had benefited each of these areas prior to 1962.

I began a long, arduous search of statistical information, information obtained primarily from federal cabinet level agencies (Departments of Health and Human Services, Justice, Education, Labor, Commerce, etc.). With the aid of dedicated co-workers, we searched through literally thousands of articles and documents relating to the four areas. The results of that search, as will be evident, are both clear and shocking.

While I initially saw the removal of school prayer as the cause for the decline, I now know that there was much more involved. As the Court has explained in no less than ten different cases:

Prayer is the quintessential religious practice. [1]

Prayer, an acknowledgment of God, is the simplest identification of a philosophy which recognizes not only the God of heaven, but also His laws and standards of conduct. Prayer, being the "heart" of religion, was by necessity the first target of an attack on religious principles. Once the heart is gone, it is merely a matter of formality to dispose of the remainder of the structure. The removal of school prayer was simply the *first* manifestation of a new Court agenda to remove *every* religious principle (and the traditional values derived from them) from public affairs.

It would have been impossible for the Court to have left school prayer intact in 1962 and then in 1980 to deliver the *Stone v. Gramm* ruling stating that it was illegal for students to view copies of the Ten Commandments. The removal of school prayer was the judicial "toe-hold" needed to extract the beliefs which had long been held as fundamental to education.

After the removal of prayer, there soon followed cases rejecting the Bible and any values derived from them—the Ten Commandments, the teaching of pre-marital sexual abstinence to students, etc. The removal of prayer was the first step on the infamous "slippery slope." While the removal of school prayer cannot be blamed for all the declines, the presence or absence, legality or illegality, of such prayers in public arenas *is* the primary indicator of the philosophy under which official public policy is being conducted.

Because prayer, the simplest expression of a belief in or recognition of God, was the most important obstacle in the war against religious principles, the return of school prayer is essential—as you will soon see on the subsequent pages. When there is an official recognition of prayer—"the quintessential religious practice"—there is also an embracing of the values and teachings of which prayer is a primary indicator. The return of school prayer will be a signal that the first step has been taken not only toward recognizing God, but toward returning His system upon which our traditional moral, ethical, and disciplinary standards are based.

David Barton
May 1991

Introduction

The heritage of this nation is one that, historically, is undeniably intertwined with religion. From the times of the Spanish explorers to the Pilgrims, from the Colonists through the Civil War and long after, religion has had a strong, positive influence on our history and on the successful development of this nation. As explained in *Compton's Encyclopedia:*

> The most powerful single influence in all history has been Christianity. This influence has shown itself not only in the religious beliefs and spiritual ideals of the human race, but in the march of political events and institutions as well. [1]

We are surrounded with recognitions of religion's positive influence on our nation: our National Anthem reflects our reliance on God; our coins declare our faith in God; and our Pledge of Allegiance heralds our testimony to God's importance in this nation. Supreme Court decisions have affirmed the religious faith of this nation:

> In 1892 the United States Supreme Court made an exhaustive study of the supposed connection between Christianity and the government of the United States. After reviewing hundreds of volumes of historical documents, the Court asserted, "These references...add a volume of unofficial declarations to the mass of organic utterances that this is a religious people...a Christian nation." Likewise, in 1931 Supreme Court Justice George Sutherland reviewed the 1892 decision in reference to another case and reiterated that Americans are a "Christian people." And in 1952 Justice William O. Douglas affirmed that "we are a religious people and our institutions presuppose a Supreme Being." [2]

Despite the extended history of the inclusion of God in the affairs of this nation, by decisions handed down on June 25, 1962, and on June 17, 1963, the Supreme Court forbade the inclusion of God in major activities of daily life. Through the cases *Engel v. Vitale, Murray v. Curlett,* and *Abington v. Schempp,* the Supreme Court forbade the free exercise of voluntary prayer or Bible reading in public schools. Never before in the history of our nation had *any* branch of our government taken such a stand.

For centuries in America, there had been an inseparable relationship between God and American public education. Our nation's first schools began in churches and for more than three centuries, public schools not only promoted prayer, they relied on the Bible as the primary instrument to teach reading, character, and morals. Students from these public schools were well-rounded and well-equipped, educated both in mind and in character. Noah Webster, a Founding Father and a founding educator, accurately reflected the nation's beliefs when he stated:

> The moral principles and precepts contained in the scriptures ought to form the basis of all our civil consti-tutions and laws...All the miseries and evils which men suffer from vice, crime, ambition, injustice, oppression, slavery, and war, proceed from their despising or neglecting the precepts contained in the Bible. [3]

Our nation, from its inception, had believed in the power and results of prayer and had strongly supported its inclusion in public arenas. Revered national political leaders, men such as George Washington and Benjamin Franklin, believed that prayer could and would change the course of the nation. They declared that this nation must include religious principles in all aspects of its national life if it were to maintain prosperity and success, either in its internal or external affairs. The Constitutional Convention of 1787 provided a vivid illustration of their conviction and leadership.

The early portion of the Constitutional Convention had been marred by dissension, hopeless deadlocks, and each state's unyielding adherence to its own selfish desires. The Convention manifested all the markings of a complete failure. A portion of the New York delegation had already departed in disgust and other delegations were preparing to follow. Even to a casual observer, it was obvious that from this setting no profitable or lasting solution to our young nation's uncertain future would be found. It was during this impasse that the nation's elder statesman and patriarch, Ben Franklin, rose to speak and quietly said:

> In the beginning of the contest with Britain, when we were sensible of danger, we had daily prayers in this room for Divine protection. Our prayers, Sir, were heard, and they were graciously answered. All of us who were engaged in the struggle must have observed frequent instances of a super-intending Providence in our favor...And have we now forgotten this powerful Friend? Or do we imagine we no longer need His assistance?
>
> I have lived, Sir, a long time, and the longer I live, the more convincing proofs I see of this truth: "that God governs in the affairs of man." And if a sparrow cannot fall to the ground without His notice, is it probable that an empire can rise without His aid?
>
> We have been assured, Sir, in the Sacred Writings that except the Lord build the house, they labor in vain that build it. I firmly believe this. *I also believe that without His concurring aid, we shall succeed in the political building no better than the builders of Babel;* we shall be divided by our little, partial local interests; our projects will be confounded; and we ourselves shall become a reproach and a byword down to future ages. And what is worse, mankind may hereafter from this unfortunate instance, despair of establishing government by human wisdom and leave it to chance, war, or conquest.
>
> *I therefore beg leave to move that, henceforth, prayers imploring the assistance of Heaven and its blessing on our deliberation be held in this assembly every morning before we proceed to business.* [4]

Franklin's rebuff rearranged the priorities of the delegates— they indeed did stop to pray. They adjourned, and for almost three days they prayed, attended church, and listened to ministers challenge and inspire them. Did those three days have any effect on the Convention? Did the prayer make any difference? According to private writings of delegates who attended the Convention, those three days were the turning point in the success of their deliberations. When they reassembled, delegate Jonathan Dayton explained:

> Every unfriendly feeling had been expelled, and a spirit of reconciliation had been cultivated. [5]

After failing in their previous efforts, and then having heeded Franklin's rebuke, how successful were they after reconvening?

> "We, the people of the United States..." Thus begins what has become the oldest written constitution still in effect today...the greatest legal minds of two centuries have continued to marvel at it as being almost beyond the scope and dimension of human wisdom. When one stops to consider the enormous problems the Constitution somehow anticipated and the challenges and testings it foresaw, that statement appears more understated than exaggerated. For not even the collective genius of the fledgling United States of America could claim credit for the fantastic strength, resilience, balance, and timelessness of the Constitution. And most of them knew it. [6]

Our brilliant Constitution and its Bill of Rights, the basis for our on-going Union, could not have come out of the selfish, dissent-filled atmosphere that first pervaded the Convention; the meeting would have failed had not Franklin stood and called for prayer. The success of both the Convention and the subsequent Constitution was the direct result of the delegates turning to prayer "every morning before proceeding to business." (It was Franklin's speech which led to the establishment of Chaplains in the House and the Senate for the purpose of offering daily prayer "every morning before proceeding to business").

George Washington also avidly believed in the importance of prayer. The Father of Our Country is remembered as a man who relied on prayer. Numerous paintings show him in prayer; even the stained glass in the U.S. Congressional Chapel portrays him kneeling in prayer. After his selection as the first President of the United States, he told Congress in his Inaugural Address:

> It would be peculiarly improper to omit, in this first official act, my fervent supplication to that Almighty Being, who rules over the universe, who presides in the councils of nations, and whose providential aids can supply every human defect, that His benediction may consecrate to the liberties and happiness of the people of the United States...No people can be bound to acknowledge and adore the invisible hand which conducts the affairs of men more than the people of the United States. Every step by which they have advanced to the character of an independent nation seems to have been distinguished by some token of providential agency....We ought to be no less persuaded that the propitious smiles of Heaven can never be expected on a nation that disregards the eternal rules of order and right, which Heaven itself has ordained. [7]

For eight years Washington wisely and skillfully guided this nation to a position from which its continued strength and development would be assured. In his Farewell Address, he warned:

> *Of all the dispositions and habits which lead to political prosperity, religion and morality are indispensable supports.* In vain would that man claim the tribute of Patriotism, who should labour to subvert these great pillars of human happiness...The mere Politician, equally with the pious man ought to respect and to cherish them...And let us with caution indulge the supposition that morality can be maintained without religion. Whatever may be conceded to the influence of refined

education on minds of peculiar structure, *reason and experience both forbid us to expect that national morality can prevail in exclusion of religious principle.* [8]

Franklin warned the nation that the exclusion of God would result in internal disputes, the decay of the nation's prestige and reputation, and a diminished national success. Washington warned that if religious principles were excluded, the nation's morality and political prosperity would suffer. Nevertheless, the Supreme Court, in only twelve months, divorced this nation's schools and public affairs from more than three centuries of its heritage! The Court had torn out part of the national fabric of American life. We are now learning experientially what both Washington and Franklin knew to be true; America is suffering in the very areas they predicted.

Chapter 1
1962—A New Direction For America

Our nation is experiencing a rapidly moving cultural revolution; practices and traditions legal for centuries recently have been declared unconstitutional. For example, in 1962-1963, 39 million students and over 2 million teachers were barred from doing what had been done since our nation's founding: pray in school.

Even today, hundreds of thousands of Americans personally recall when prayer, Bible reading, and religious principles were as much a part of their public school education as was the study of math or the pursuit of athletics. Activities once thought to be an integral part of education now are totally separated.

The sudden and dramatic restructuring of educational policies was precipitated by the Court's reinterpretation of "separation of church and state." The First Amendment (which actually states, "Congress shall make no law respecting an establishment of religion, or prohibiting the free exercise thereof") had always meant that Congress was prohibited from establishing a national religious denomination—that Congress could not require that all Americans become Catholics, Anglicans, or members of any other denomination. This understanding of "separation of church and state" was applied not only during the time of the Founders, but for 170 years afterwards.

Then, in 1962, the Supreme Court changed the definition of "church." No longer would "church" mean a "denomination"; instead, "church" now would mean a "religious activity." Therefore, "separation of church and state" suddenly meant the complete separation of any religious activity from public affairs.

This new definition of "church" immediately invited hundreds of lawsuits challenging any presence of religion in public life. While skyrocketing numbers of lawsuits are still awaiting disposition in court dockets, the courts have already delivered far-reaching decisions to:

Remove student prayer: "Prayer in its public school system breaches the constitutional wall of separation between Church and State." [1] *(Engel v. Vitale, 1962)*

Remove school Bible readings: "If portions of the New Testament were read without explanation, they could be, and...had been, psychologically harmful to the child." [2] *(Abington v. Schempp, 1963)*

Remove the Ten Commandments from view: "If the posted copies of the Ten Commandments are to have any effect at all, it will be to induce the schoolchildren to read, meditate upon, perhaps to venerate and obey, the Commandments...this...is not a permissible state objective under the Establishment Clause...The mere posting of the copies [of the Ten Commandments]... the [First Amendment] prohibits." [3] *(Stone v. Gramm, 1980)*

Remove benedictions and invocations from school activities: "Religious invocation...in high school commencement exercise conveyed message that district had given its endorsement to prayer and religion, so that school district was properly [prohibited] from including invocation in commencement exercise." *(Graham v. Central, 1985)* [4] *(Kay v. Douglas, 1986)* [5] *(Jager v. Douglas, 1989)* [6]

Remove the word "God" from school correspondence: "To include reference to God...would violate...First Amendment." [7] *(Ohio v. Whisner, 1976)*

The Court's new interpretation of the First Amendment in 1962 was so unprecedented that the 1970 *Walz* Court was forced to acknowledge that the reinterpretation of the First Amendment had been used "for only a few decades at best" and that:

It was...*not until 1962* that...prayers were held to violate the [First Amendment]. [8]

Later Courts confirmed that fact. The 1962 *Engel v. Vitale* case removing voluntary student prayer was the watershed case—the turning point. The decision by the Court to remove prayer had been made without *any* previous precedent, either legal *or* historical. The Court argued that it needed no precedent because "everyone" understood that there was to be no religious principles in schools:

> Finally, in Engel v. Vitale, only last year, these principles [the separation of religious principles from education] were so *universally recognized* that the Court, *without the citation of a single case*...reaffirmed them. [9]

The 1962-63 separation of Christian principles from education was something so new and totally different that it brought comment from national observers. The *1963 World Book Encyclopedia Yearbook* stated:

> The significance of the decision regarding this [school] prayer was enormous, for the whole thorny problem of religion in public education *was thus inevitably raised.* [10]

Prior to 1962, according to the *World Book,* the legal issue of separating religious principles from education had not been "raised." Legal observers also noted the Court's new posture:

> *The Court has broken new ground* in a number of fields....Few Supreme Court decisions of recent years have created greater furor than *Engel v. Vitale.* [11]

Before the 1962 *Engel* decision, the unwavering position held by the Court since its rulings in the 1700's was described in the 1952 *Zorach v. Clauson* case:

> The First Amendment, however, does not say that in every and all respects there shall be a separation of Church and State...Otherwise the state and religion would be aliens to each other—hostile, suspicious, and even unfriendly. [12]

Nevertheless, only ten years after that statement, the Court repudiated 170 years of Supreme Court rulings and ordered the removal of all religious activities from public schools. Since 1962-1963, the Court has taken great strides to strengthen the legal philosophy it pioneered—it has handed down many additional rulings further restricting a student's access to, much less observance of, religious principles. Lower court rulings have gone even further than those of the Supreme Court, chipping away at the original intent until a religion-hostile position is now taken toward *any* exposure to religious principles in most public schools.

How could the 1962 Supreme Court Justices have ignored such a lengthy Court history which protected Christian principles in public education? Why did they so readily repudiate so many previous rulings? Perhaps the answer rests in the fact that of the 1962-63 Supreme Court Justices, eight of the nine had arrived on the Court with an extended history of *political* experience, *not* judicial experience.

For example, Chief Justice Earl Warren had been the Governor of California for ten years prior to his appointment to the Court; Justice Hugo Black had been a U.S. Senator for ten years prior to his appointment; Justice Felix Frankfurter had been an assistant to the Secretary of Labor and a founding member of the ACLU; Justice Arthur Goldberg had been the Secretary of Labor and Ambassador to the United Nations; Justice William Douglas was chairman of the Securities and Exchange Commission prior to his appointment; all the Justices except Potter Stewart had similar political backgrounds.

Justice Potter Stewart, having been a federal judge for four years prior to his appointment, was the *only* member of the Court with extended federal Constitutional experience *before* his appointment. Interestingly, Justice Potter Stewart was also the only Justice who objected to the removal of prayer and Bible reading. He alone acted as a judge; the rest acted as politicians, determined to develop new policies rather than uphold previous precedents.

Those Justices not only initiated the anti-Christian policy, they firmly guided and strengthened it during their tenure. Today, there is such prejudice against religion in public arenas that courts have declared:

- Freedom of speech and press is guaranteed to students unless the topic is religious, at which time such speech becomes unconstitutional. [13]
- If a student prays over his lunch, it is unconstitutional for him to pray aloud. [14]
- It is unconstitutional for a Board of Education to use or refer to the word "God" in any of its official writings. [15]

Furthermore:

- Public schools were barred from showing a film about the settlement of Jamestown because the film depicted the erection of a cross at the settlement, despite the historical fact that a cross *was* erected at the Jamestown settlement. [16]
- In the Alaska public schools, students were told they could not use the word "Christmas" in school because it had the word "Christ" in it, nor could they have the word in their notebooks, nor exchange Christmas cards or presents, nor display anything with the word "Christmas" on it. [17]
- In Virginia, a federal court has ruled that a homosexual newspaper may be distributed on a high school campus, but religious newspapers may not. [18]
- In Colorado, a music teacher was stopped from singing traditional Christmas carols in her classes. [19]

What occurs in the classroom is of vital significance to the rest of the nation. As explained by President Abraham Lincoln:

The philosophy of the class room in one generation will be the philosophy of government in the next. [20]

———— • • • ————

Although the chaos in education readily demonstrates the effects which have occurred since the separation of religious principles from public affairs, those effects are by no means limited solely to education. The Court's removal of religious principles has also caused the reversal of long-standing social policies on children, families, and the nation. Each of these areas had been able to boast of an extended legal history in which the Court not only refused to separate religious principles, but had relied on those principles when rendering its decisions. The following statements are representative of those which appeared in scores of earlier cases:

> Christianity has reference to the principles of right and wrong...it is the foundation of those morals and manners upon which our society is formed; it is their basis. Remove this and they would fall...[morality] has grown upon the basis of Christianity....The day of moral virtue in which we live would, in an instant, if that standard were abolished, lapse into the dark and murky night of Pagan immorality. [21] *Charleston v. Benjamin*

> The morality of the country is deeply engrafted upon Christianity...[we are] people whose manners...and whose morals have been elevated and inspired...by means of the Christian religion. [22] *People v. Ruggles*

The subsequent chapters present clear and compelling evidence of the extensive damage caused by the removal of Christian principles from public affairs in 1962-63.

Let it be stressed that the removal of school prayer was **not** singly the culprit for all of the nation's ills—an instant return of school prayer will **not** provide a magical cure. The rejection of school prayer was merely the primary indication of a new guiding philosophy, a new Court-imposed hostility toward religion. As the Court explained in *Jaffree v. Wallace* (and in nine other cases):

> Prayer is the quintessential religious practice. [23]

Since prayer is the most obvious expression of religious principles, by necessity it was the first target of the war against religious principles in public affairs. School prayer, a mere acknowledgment of God, is the simplest identification of a philosophy which recognizes not only the God of heaven, but also His laws and standards of conduct.

For example, where prayer is found, one is not surprised also to find the Bible, the Ten Commandments, a nativity scene, etc.; where there is an absence of prayer, it is not surprising that there is also an absence of Biblical principles or values. In fact, it would be surprising to find religious values present where prayer is absent.

It would have been impossible for the Court to have left school prayer intact in 1962 and then in 1980 to deliver the *Stone v. Gramm* ruling stating that it was illegal for students to view copies of the Ten Commandments. The removal of school prayer was the judicial "toe-hold" needed to extract the beliefs which long had been held as fundamental to education.

When the Supreme Court prohibited school prayer on June 25, 1962, it achieved the unenviable notoriety of becoming the first governmental entity since the birth of the nation to forbid prayer in a public forum. While school prayers varied among districts (some used extemporaneous prayers, others the Lord's Prayer, the 23rd Psalm, or prayers approved by the local school board), most contained the basic elements of the 22-word prayer struck down in *Engel v. Vitale:*

> *Almighty God, we acknowledge our dependence upon Thee, and we beg Thy blessings upon us, our parents, our teachers and our Country.* [24]

That simple prayer serves as the basic outline for this book. The prayer for *"us"* (the students themselves), *"our parents"* (their families), *"our teachers"* (their academic leaders), and *"our Country"* (our nation) identifies the four categories of documentation in this work. Through the use of statistical information gathered primarily from U.S. governmental offices, the years when religious principles guided our national policies in each of these areas will be contrasted with the years following their expulsion.

Chapter 2
"Us"—The Youth

George Washington, in his Farewell Address (perhaps the most significant political speech ever delivered by a U.S. President), warned the nation:

> And let us with caution indulge the supposition that morality may be maintained without religion. Whatever may be conceded to the influence of refined education on minds...reason and experience both forbid us to expect that national morality can prevail in exclusion of religious principle. [1]

Washington's statement was not a radical new teaching; it was the articulation of a fundamental and commonly held belief of the Founders. Not merely reason, but experience had proven that morality could *not* be maintained if separated from religious principles. This was also the unquestioned and unalterable stand in Supreme Court rulings for 170 years until the Court arbitrarily rejected those standards in 1962.

So completely have religious principles been expunged from education that in 1981, a court ruled on a legal challenge against teaching pre-marital sexual abstinence to students in public schools. Notice excerpts from the court's decision:

> The harm of premarital sexual relations...are fundamental elements of religious doctrine. It is a fundamental tenet of many religions that premarital sex...[is] wrong....
>
> In short, the [program teaching pre-marital sexual abstinence] has the primary effect of advancing religion. This alone would force the court to declare the law constitutionally infirm....
>
> [T]he inescapable conclusion is that federal funds have been used...to teach matters inherently tied to religion. [2]
> *Kendrick v. Bowen*

Although this case was eventually modified by the Supreme Court in 1988, the fact that it even reached the Court, and that it took 7 years to reach a partial resolution, shows the extent to which basic moral values have been rejected under the new interpretation of separation of church and state.

In 1988, California was considering adopting legislation on sex-education for public schools requiring that:

Course material and instruction shall stress that monogamous heterosexual intercourse [one man and one woman] within marriage is a traditional American value.

The Senator promoting the bill received a letter of protest from the ACLU dated April 18, 1988:

It is our position that monogamous, heterosexual intercourse within marriage as a traditional American value is an unconstitutional establishment of a religious doctrine in public schools. There are various religions which hold contrary beliefs with respect to marriage and monogamy. We believe [this bill] violates the First Amendment.

Students across the nation are being provided with materials in their sex-education classes from groups like *Planned Parenthood*—materials containing photographs, illustrations, and graphics encouraging and demonstrating pre-marital sexual relations for adolescents. Consider these "mild" excerpts from books and materials that *Planned Parenthood* and similar groups recommend for adolescents: [3]

Boys and Sex: [4]

More and more people are coming to understand that having sex is a joyful and enriching experience at any age. (p. 2)

Playing with girls sexually before adolescence... increases the chances for a satisfactory sex life when a boy grows up. (p. 38)

Premarital intercourse does have its definite values as a training ground for marriage...boys and girls who start having intercourse when they're adolescents...will find that it's a big help...it's like taking a car out on a test run before you buy it. (p. 117)

Girls and Sex: [5]

Girls understand now that they are far more likely to make good social and sexual adjustments to life if they learn to be warm, open, responsive, and sexually unafraid. They're learning to be sexual partners of men. (p. 10-11)

Everyone's agreed...that teenage sex should be a learning experience. (p. 15)

Sex play with boys...can be exciting, pleasurable, and even worthwhile...it will help later sexual adjustment. (p. 48)

You've Changed the Combination: [6]

There are only two basic kinds of sex: sex with victims and sex without. Sex with victims is always wrong. Sex without is always right....One way to avoid having victims is, of course, to have sexual relationships only with your friends.

The Great Orgasm Robbery: [7]

Sex is fun, and joyful...and it comes in all types and styles, all of which are OK. Do what gives pleasure and enjoy what gives pleasure and ask for what gives pleasure. Don't rob yourself of joy by focusing on old-fashioned ideas about what's "normal" or "nice."

The effect that these school sex-ed curriculums have had on the nation since the rejection of religious principles is apparent. By prohibiting student access to religious principles, the Court has prohibited student access to the principles which produce morality. On the following graphs, notice the unusually strong correlation between the Courts' decisions to prohibit student access to religious principles while at school and the dramatic changes in student morality.

Birth Rates For Unwed Girls
15-19 Years Of Age

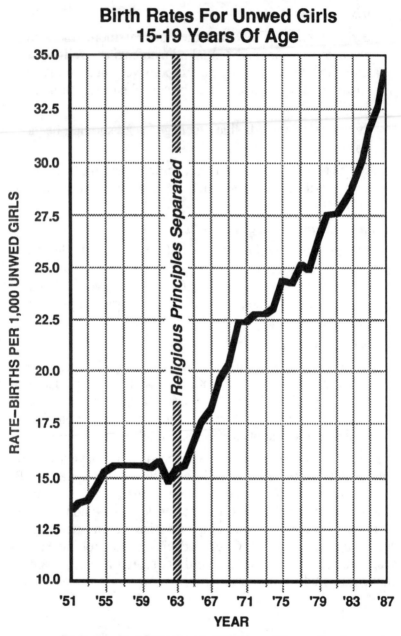

Basic data from Department of Health and Human Services and
Statistical Abstracts of the United States.

Pregnancies To Unwed Girls
Under 15 Years of Age

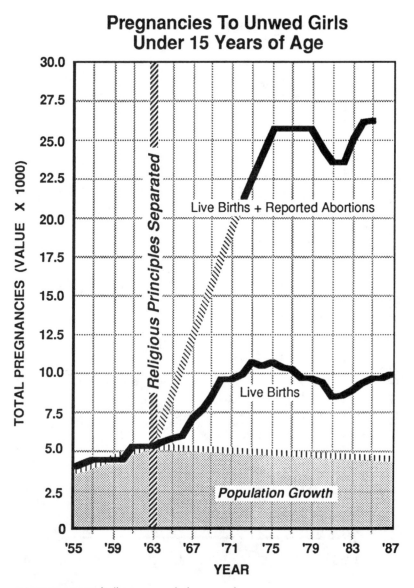

IIIIIIIIIIIIIII Indicates population growth.
\\\\\\\\\\\\\\\ Indicates interpolated data.

Basic data from Department of Health and Human Services,
Statistical Abstracts of the United States, the Center for Disease Control,
and the Department of Commerce, Census Bureau.

Pregnancies To Unwed Girls
15-19 Years Of Age

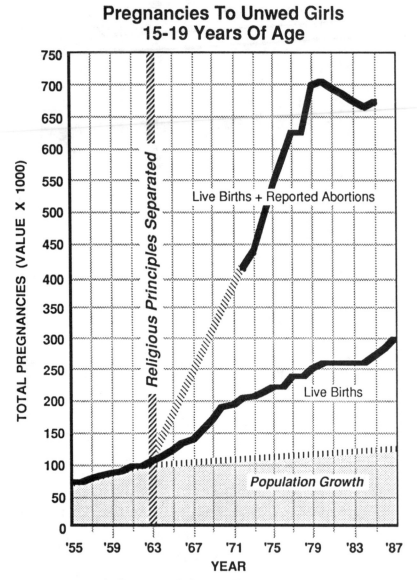

|||||||||||||||||| Indicates population growth.
⌇⌇⌇⌇⌇⌇⌇⌇⌇⌇⌇⌇ Indicates interpolated data.

Basic data from Department of Health and Human Services,
Statistical Abstracts of the United States, the Center for Disease Control,
and the Department of Commerce, Census Bureau.

(*Information on Teen Pregnancies*)

Since the Court-ordered removal of religious principles in 1962:

- The United States has the highest incidence of teenage motherhood of any Western country. [8]
- Each year, 1 million adolescent girls become pregnant. Of those who give birth, half are not yet 18. [9]
- 80 percent of pregnant teenage girls are unmarried. [10]
- The birth rate for unmarried teens rose an additional 14 percent from 1980 to 1985, following an increase of 18 percent during the 1970's. [11]
- Teenage motherhood among school students is so prevalent that a Dallas *high school* established a 15-bed nursery for students with children[12] and Houston has dedicated two entire high-schools for the same purpose. [13]

The impact of teen pregnancies in educational and economic areas is substantial:

- In 1985 alone, $16.65 billion was paid through welfare to women who gave birth as teenagers. [14] In 1990, the cost had risen to $20.6 billion. [15]
- Of those families headed by a mother age 14-25, two-thirds live below the poverty level. [16]
- Of the 1.3 million children of teenage mothers, 804,000 are currently in need of day care. [17]
- Only half of those who give birth before age 18 complete high school (as compared with 96 percent of those who postpone childbearing), they earn half as much money, and are far more likely to be dependent on welfare (71 percent of women under 30 who receive aid had their first child as a teenager, i.e., during the late 60's and early- to mid-70's). [18]

(*Sexually Transmitted Diseases*)

The changes in student morality since the separation of religious principles is also evident in measurements showing cases of sexually transmitted diseases among students:

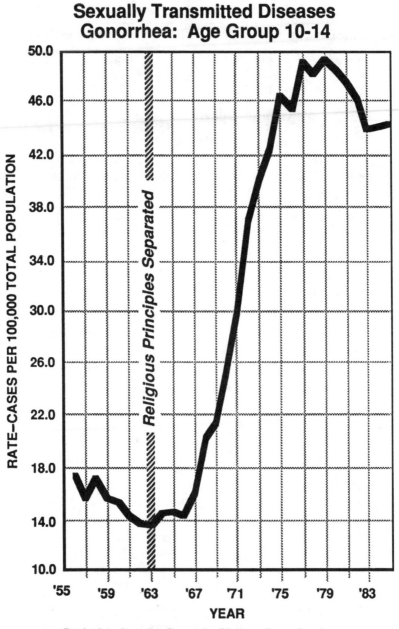

Sexually Transmitted Diseases
Gonorrhea: Age Group 10-14

Basic data from the Center for Disease Control and
Department of Health and Human Resources.

Sexually Transmitted Diseases
Gonorrhea: Age Group 15-19

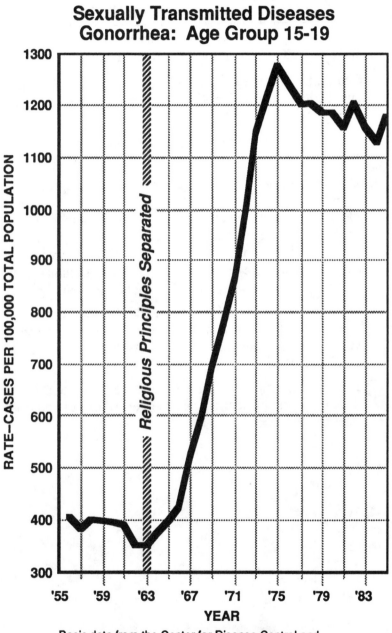

Basic data from the Center for Disease Control and
Department of Health and Human Resources.

Information on Student Sexual Activity

What has happened to sexual activity among students since they have been denied access to Christian principles?

- Two-thirds of America's 11 million teenage boys say they have had sex with a girl...By the time they are 18, on the average, boys have had sex with five girls. [19]

- Most boys had their first sexual experience at 14 and girls at age 15. [20]

- Of those students who have gone through a comprehensive sex education program, 65 percent are sexually active, a percentage almost twice as high as those who have *not* completed a sex-education curriculum. Additionally, 42 percent of those who have never been in a comprehensive sex education class (which promotes "promiscuous intercourse of the sexes") have not had sexual intercourse. [21]

- According to the Sex Information and Education Council of the U.S. (SIECUS), one out of every two boys and one of every three girls between the ages of 15 and 17 have had sexual intercourse.

The following graphs indicate the upsurge in promiscuous sexual activity among teens since the separation of religious principles in 1962-63:

Premarital Sexual Activity
Among U.S. Teenage Girls
Age 15

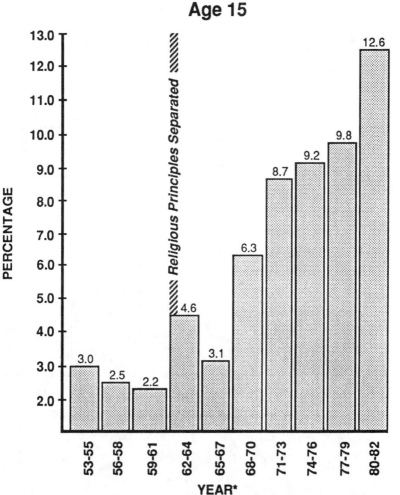

*The year in which the subject age group turned 15. Information was available in three (3) year groupings only. Table shows the percentage of U.S. 15 yr. old teenage girls who have had premarital intercourse.

Basic data from *Family Planning Perspectives*, Vol. 19, No. 2, March/April 1987.
Furnished by the Alan Guttmacher Institute

Premarital Sexual Activity
Among U.S. Teenage Girls
Age 16

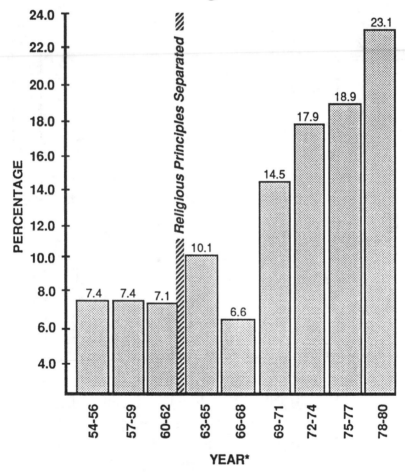

* The year in which the subject age group turned 16. Information was available in three (3) year groupings only. Table shows the percentage of U.S. 16 yr. old teenage girls who have had premarital intercourse.

Basic data from *Family Planning Perspectives,*
Vol. 19, No. 2, March/April 1987.
Furnished by the Alan Guttmacher Institute

Premarital Sexual Activity
Among U.S. Teenage Girls
Age 17

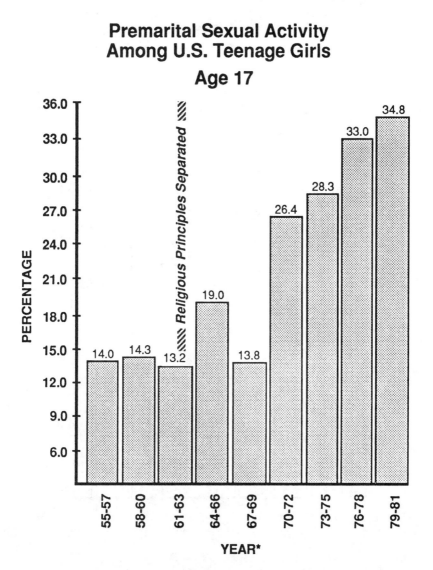

* The year in which the subject age group turned 17. Information was available in three (3) year groupings only. Table shows the percentage of U.S. 17 yr. old teenage girls who have had premarital intercourse.

Basic data from *Family Planning Perspectives*,
Vol. 19, No. 2, March/April 1987.
Furnished by the Alan Guttmacher Institute

Premarital Sexual Activity
Among U.S. Teenage Girls
Age 18

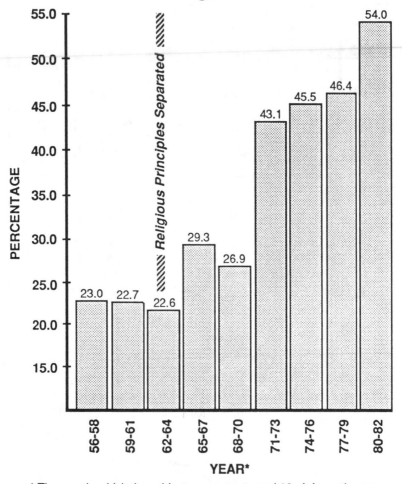

* The year in which the subject age group turned 18. Information was available in three (3) year groupings only. Table shows the percentage of U.S. 18 yr. old teenage girls who have had premarital intercourse.

Basic data from *Family Planning Perspectives,*
Vol. 19, No. 2, March/April 1987.
Furnished by the Alan Guttmacher Institute

Pre-Marital Sex

Percentage of U.S. Teenage Girls
Who Have Had Pre-Marital Intercourse

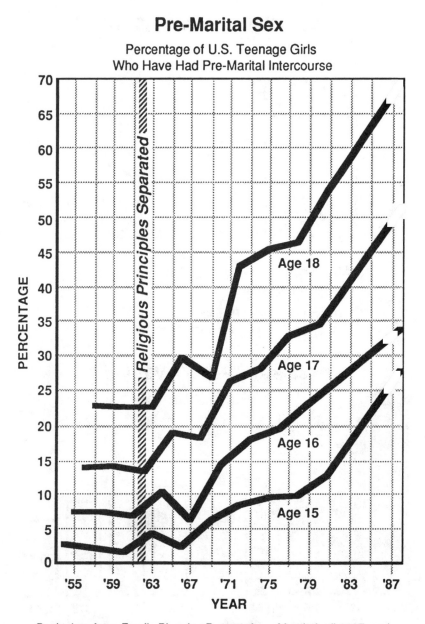

Basic data from *Family Planning Perspectives,* March/April 1987, and from *Sexual and Reproductive Behavior of American Women, 1982-88.* Furnished by the Alan Guttmacher Institute.

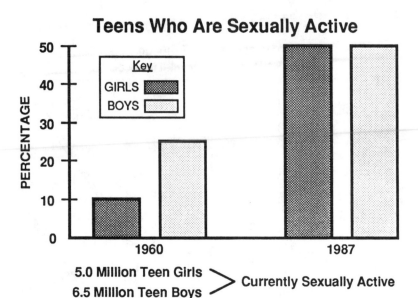

Teens Who Are Sexually Active

Key
GIRLS
BOYS

5.0 Million Teen Girls
6.5 Million Teen Boys
> Currently Sexually Active

"Teenagers and Sex," *Parents,* January 1987, p.127.
"Young and Pregnant," *Parents,* March 1987, p. 196.

Male and Female Virgins
on a College Campus

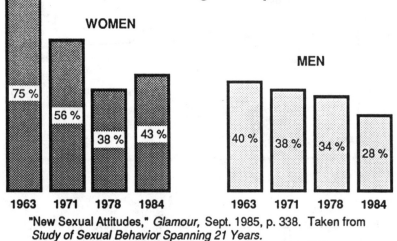

WOMEN

MEN

75 %
56 %
38 %
43 %
40 %
38 %
34 %
28 %

1963   1971   1978   1984   1963   1971   1978   1984

"New Sexual Attitudes," *Glamour,* Sept. 1985, p. 338. Taken from
Study of Sexual Behavior Spanning 21 Years.
Robert Sherwin and Sherry Corbett, Miami University, Ohio.

Information on the sexual attitudes held by youth today was provided by the Rhode Island Rape Crisis Center in a survey of 1,700 sixth- through ninth-grade students (approximate ages of 12-15) in eight cities. [22]   In one question, the students were asked: "Under which situations does a man have a right to intercourse *against a woman's consent?*"   The question described rape without using that particular word; as shown below, the students' responses were both revealing and shocking:

Students' Attitudes Toward Rape		
Category	Percentages*	
It is okay for a man to force a woman to have sex against her consent if...	Boys	Girls
...he has been dating her for 6 to 12 months	65%	47%
...he spends as much as $10 to $15 on her	24%	16%
...they are planning to get married	74%	67%
...she had done it with other men	31%	32%

* The numbers in each column indicate the percentage of students who agreed with the statement.

Though the stipulations varied, nearly one-half the students felt that there *were* conditions which authorized rape. With so many "situations" justifying rape—with so many attitudes condoning it—the guarantee of a "safe" date no longer exists. Jackson Kikuchi, coordinator for the adolescent awareness program for the center conducting the research, declared:

> So many of our kids have attitudes that sexual abuse is okay. I would...not have thought that 12- and 13-year-olds would think it's okay for a guy to force them to have intercourse with them. Such attitudes are probably triggering date rape and other forms of sexual assault. National statistics state that at least 25 percent of the girls in this country will be sexually assaulted before they turn 18. [23]

Sixty-two percent of whose who reported sexual assaults in 1986 reported that the assault was date or acquaintance rape. That almost two-thirds of the attacks came from "friends" shows that self-indulgence has become the attitude of the day—gratify yourself no matter what the consequence to others.

The atrocious attitudes displayed in this study proceed directly from despising and/or ignoring the fundamental religious principles openly taught in schools prior to 1962. As Noah Webster explained:

> All the miseries and evils which men suffer from vice, crime, ambition, injustice, oppression, slavery, and war, proceed from their despising or neglecting the precepts contained in the Bible. [24]

It is ironic that the Court allows students to be exposed to teachings which promote sexual activity but forbids them access to Christian teachings which promote self-control and internal restraints. George Washington's warning again seems pertinent:

> And let us with caution indulge the supposition that morality can be maintained without religion. Whatever may be conceded to the influence of refined education on minds...*reason and experience both forbid us to expect that national morality can prevail in exclusion of religious principle.* [25]

Since the Court excluded Christian principles from students at schools, premarital sexual activity among 15 year old students has increased almost 500% [26] with half of sexually active males having had their first sexual experience between the ages of 11 and 13;[27] sexually transmitted diseases (i.e., gonorrhea) have increased over 200%; and teenage student pregnancies have increased over 400%,[28] causing the United States to become the Western World's leader in teenage pregnancies,[29] with one-and-a-quarter million adolescent pregnancies each year. [30]

Indeed, true to warnings by Washington, the other Founders, and the pre-1962 Courts, it is evident that widespread morality

Chapter 3
"Our Parents"—The Family

The lives of students have changed dramatically since the removal of religious principles from schools; the changes in families have been no less dramatic. A review of Court cases prior to 1963 will emphasize the magnitude of the turnaround; the Court's dealings with families, just as with students, had always been based on traditional Biblical standards. Notice these representative rulings:

> Marriage was not originated by human law. When God created Eve, she was a wife to Adam; they then and there occupied the status of husband to wife and wife to husband...When Noah was selected for salvation from the flood, he and his wife and his three sons and their wives were placed in the Ark; and, when the flood waters had subsided and the families came forth, it was Noah and his wife and each son and his wife...The truth is that civil government has grown out of marriage...which created homes, and population, and society, from which government became necessary....[Marriages] will produce a home and family that will contribute to good society, to free and just government, and to the support of Christianity...It would be sacrilegious to apply the designation "a civil contract" to such a marriage. It is that and more; a status ordained by God. [1] *Grigsby v. Reib*

> [Marriage] is the most solemn and important of human transactions. It is regarded by all Christian nations as the basis of civilized society, of sound morals, and of the domestic affections...The mutual comfort and happiness of the parties are the principal, but not the only, objects of the [marriage]. It is intended also for the benefit of their common offspring, and is an important element in the moral order, security and tranquility of civilized society. The parties cannot dissolve the contract, as they can others, by mutual consent, and no light or trivial

causes should be suffered to effect its recision... according to the experience of the most enlightened nations, the happiness of married life greatly depends on its indissolubility. [2] *Sheffield v. Sheffield*

Handling the family according to God's standards as revealed through the Bible long formed the heart of governmental policy toward the family. Had that long-standing policy been a good policy? George Washington, in his Farewell Address, identified the components of good public policy:

Observe good faith and justice toward all...cultivate peace and harmony with all. Religion and morality [encourage] this conduct. And can it be that good policy does not equally [include] it? [3]

In Washington's opinion, a policy cannot be a good policy unless it includes religion and morality. Nonetheless, in 1962-63, the Court adamantly rejected the previous components of good family policy. What have been the effects of rejecting a Bible-based family policy? The results are evident on the following charts.

Divorce Rates

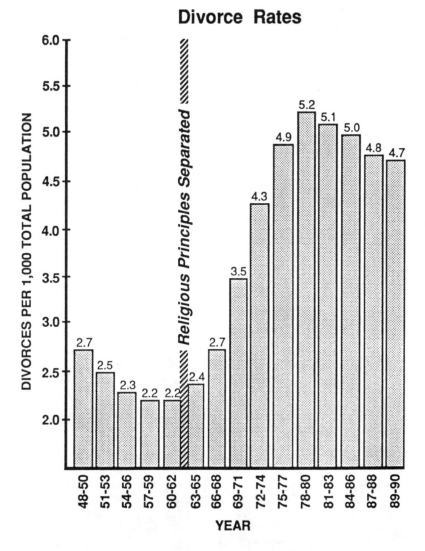

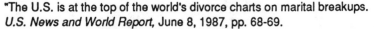

"The U.S. is at the top of the world's divorce charts on marital breakups. *U.S. News and World Report,* June 8, 1987, pp. 68-69.

"The number of divorces tripled each year between 1962 and 1981." *Time,* July 13, 1987, p. 21.

Basic data from the U. S. National Center for Health Statistics, *Vital Statistics of the United States,* annual.

Single Person Households

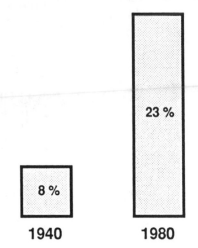

Single Parent Households
with Children

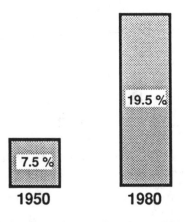

Basic data from *USA Today*, August 1985, p. 1.

Single Parent Households
Female Head, No Spouse Present

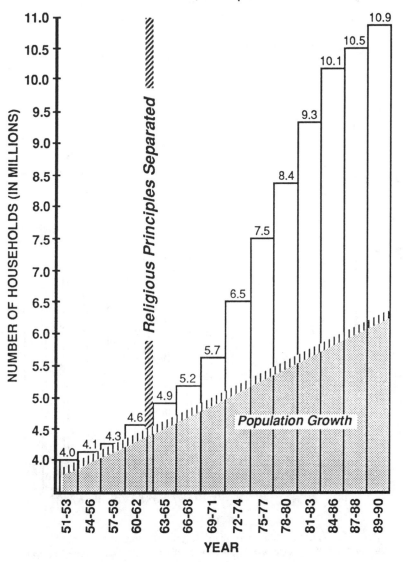

IIIIIIIIII Indicates population growth profile.

Basic data from *Statistical Abstracts of the United States,*
and the Department of Commerce, Census Bureau.

Not only has family stability markedly deteriorated since rejection of the Biblical family approach, family morality (evidenced by the numbers of unmarried couples living together and the rate of adultery) has also decayed significantly:

Unmarried Couples Living Together

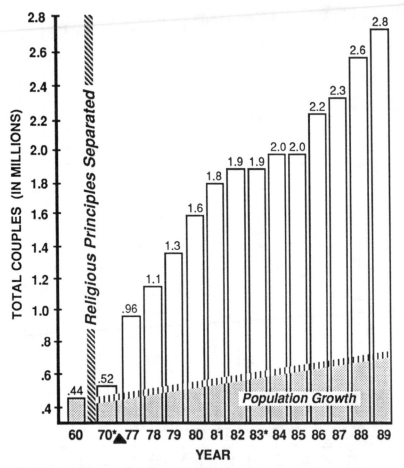

▲ Prior to 1977, unmarried couples living together was such a small group that data on this group was collected only in the 10-year census reports.

* Note: Unmarried couples represented only 1 in 85 of all couples in 1970, compared with 1 in 25 in 1983.

Basic data from *Statistical Abstracts of the United States*.

Adultery: Percentage
Involved in Extra-Marital Sex

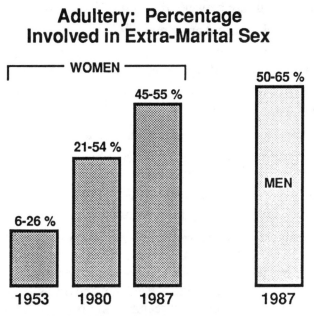

Basic data from "Unfaithfully Yours," *People,* August 18, 1986, p. 85,
research by Alfred Kinsey; and "The News About Infidelity," *Cosmopolitan,*
Apr. '87, p. 212, research by G.D. Nass, R.W. Libby, and M.P. Fisher.

The deterioration of the family following the exclusion of
religious standards from family policy is apparent: divorces
are up almost 120 percent; single parent families have
increased 140 percent; single parent families involving children
have skyrocketed 160 percent; unmarried couples living
together have increased over 350 percent; and adultery has
increased three to four times over previous levels. However,
these are not the only areas of concern for the family.

(Runaways)

Social professionals agree that the disintegration of the
family structure (by separation, divorce, etc.) is the cause of an
intensive major problem in America—runaway youth: [4]

- From 1.3 to 1.5 million children and youth run away
  from home each year. [5]

- Nearly half are between the ages of 15 and 16. [6]
- Fifty-eight percent are female. [7]
- Forty-six percent are "pushouts" (youth whose parents push them out and encourage their leaving). [8]
- More than half come from households where one or both parents are alcoholics. [9]
- Nearly one-third come from single-parent homes. [10]
- Forty-three percent cite physical abuse as an important reason for leaving home. [11]
- Seventy-three percent of runaway girls and 38 percent of boys report having been sexually abused. [12]

Also, runaways who were sexually abused are more likely to report suicidal feelings and are more likely to have trouble in school, to engage in delinquent and criminal activity, to participate in acts of violence, and to use alcohol and drugs. [13]

According to Jay Howell, director of the National Center for Missing and Exploited Children (an organization partially funded by the Justice Department): "The most dangerous place for a child in this country is in his or her home." [14]

(Summary)

The devastation of the family since the Court segregated religious principles from its dealings with families makes Washington's warning worthy of review:

> Observe good faith and justice towards all...cultivate peace and harmony with all; religion and morality [encourage] this conduct; and can it be that good policy does not equally [include] it? [15]

Can it really be a good policy if it does not encourage religion and morality? Not according to statistical indicators nor in the opinion of the Founders.

Chapter 4
"Our Teachers"—American Education

Since 1962, the Courts have delivered ruling after ruling eradicating all vestiges of religious principles from education. Notice the features once thought essential to education which are now excluded:

Prayer:

Prayer in its public school system breaches the constitutional wall of separation between Church and State. [1] *Engel v. Vitale, 1962*

Practice of having invocations delivered prior to public high school games...had the primary effect of advancing religion, and thus violated the First Amendment. [2] *Jager v. Douglas, 1989*

Bible:

If portions of the New Testament were read [to the students] they could be, and...had been, psychologically harmful to the child. [3] *Abington v. Schempp, 1963*

School district acted properly in prohibiting teacher from [silently] reading Bible [to himself] in...school classroom [during silent reading period]. [4] *Roberts v. Madigan, 1989*

Ten Commandments:

The mere posting of the copies [of the Ten Commandments]...the [First Amendment] prohibits....If the posted copies of the Ten Commandments are to have any effect at all, it will be to induce the schoolchildren to read, meditate upon, perhaps to venerate and obey, the Commandments...this...is not a permissible... objective. [5] *Stone v. Gramm, 1980*

Spiritual Heritage:

[The bill's] sponsor...intended to provide children the opportunity of sharing in their spiritual heritage of Alabama and of this country....[and] thus violates the First Amendment. [6] *Wallace v. Jaffree, 1984*

The Acknowledgment of God:

To include reference to "God"...would violate...[the] First Amendment. [7] *Ohio v. Whisner, 1976*

The removal of religious principles created a value-free environment—one free of moral absolutes or fixed rights and wrongs. The removal of moral absolutes based on religious principles has altered every aspect of student life—morality, behavior, and achievement. Numerous statistical measurements are available which indicate those changes.

Although for many categories there are statistical measurements which span decades (i.e., student achievement scores, dropout rates, high-school equivalency testing, etc.), many of the current areas of concern have few tangibles for comparing the present with the past. And understandably so, for when the American education system was sound and commanded international respect, few statistics were kept in non-problem areas.

For example, measurements on school violence and school crime rarely appeared prior to the the mid-70's; since school violence had not been a problem, few records were kept. Today that is not the case. Numerous other categories which provide little data from the past (illiteracy, teacher competency, etc.) testify that these are recent problems—problems intensifying only since the Court ordered religious principles out of education.

(The SAT Test)

One of the premier indicators of student achievement is the SAT—the Scholastic Aptitude Test. The SAT, a test measuring a student's verbal and math skills, was first administered to high-school students in 1926; in 1941 a common scale was established to allow annual comparisons of the scores. Consequently, the SAT is an invaluable resource—it remains the only major achievement test that has not been recently renormed; it has been comparing "apples with apples" since 1941. The following graphs designate the point at which religious principles were first separated from education; the consequences are evident.

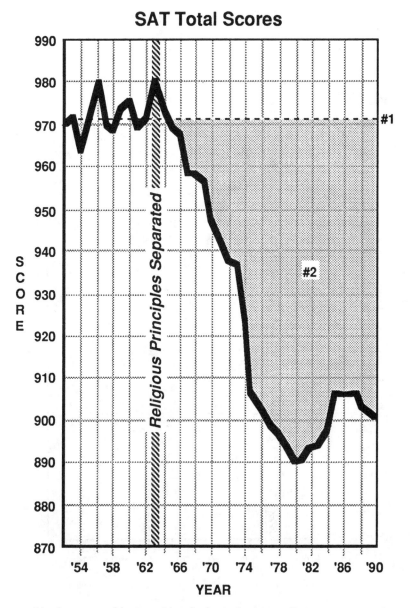

SAT Total Scores

Religious Principles Separated

#1

#2

#1 - Average achievement level prior to the separation

#2 - Amount of reduced academic achievement since the separation

Basic data from the College Entrance Exam Board.

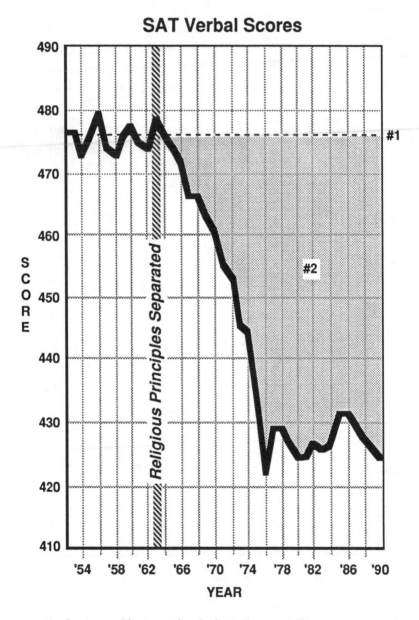

SAT Verbal Scores

#1 - Average achievement level prior to the separation
#2 - Amount of reduced academic achievement since the separation

Basic data from the College Entrance Exam Board.

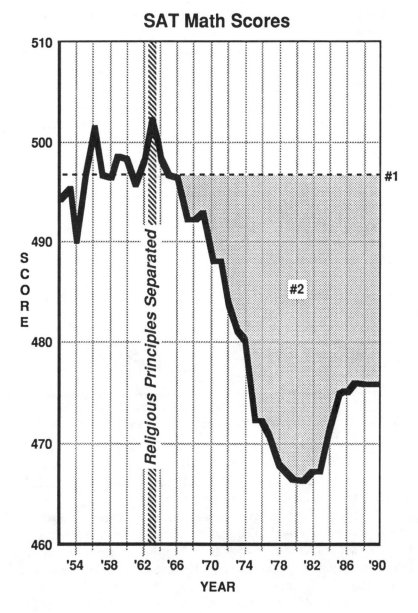

SAT Math Scores

Religious Principles Separated

#1

#2

#1 - Average achievement level prior to the separation
#2 - Amount of reduced academic achievement since the separation

Basic data from the College Entrance Exam Board.

The Court-ordered removal of religious principles from education initiated eighteen consecutive years of decline—unprecedented in the history of the SAT. Prior to 1962-63, SAT scores had not declined more than two consecutive years in a row.

Although uninterrupted declines occurred following the separation of religious principles, the rate of decline had slowed by the mid-70's, and from 1981 scores actually improved until 1987, when they again turned downward (note the graph below):

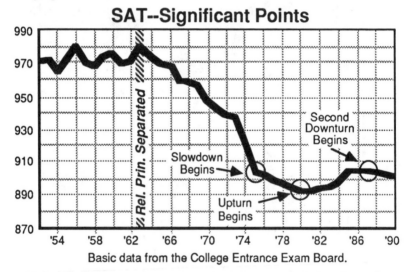

SAT--Significant Points

Basic data from the College Entrance Exam Board.

If the removal of religious principles caused the downturn, why would the decline slow in 1974-1975, and why would scores turn upward in 1981? Afterall, religious principles had not been returned to education.

In 1974-75, when the rate of decline first began to slow, a new trend had emerged in education: large numbers of private/religious schools began to appear. According to Department of Education figures, between 1974-1984, private school enrollment jumped 17 percent, reaching an enrollment of 8,465,000 students by 1984! The dramatic increase of private school students is even more remarkable when realizing that the total number of students attending school in the nation actually *decreased* between 1974-1984.

The fantastic growth in private school enrollment was primarily seen among religiously-affiliated schools. (According to the College Board, 72 percent of private-school students attend religiously-affiliated schools). As an example, Accelerated Christian Education (ACE) had 479 affiliate schools in 1974; by 1984, the number had jumped to over 6,000 schools with more than 240,000 students. The American Association of Christian Schools (AACS) represented 125 schools with 16,000 students in 1972; by 1990, that number had climbed to 1,200 schools with 165,000 students. In the Association of Christian Schools International (ACSI), the number of students in its affiliated schools increased from 186,000 in 1978 to 475,000 in 1989.

The significant growth rate in Christian schools was commented upon by several national observers. A December 20, 1984, *USA Today* article reported that enrollments at denominational schools had increased a remarkable 22 percent in the *three-year period* 1981-1984. The February 3, 1985, *Washington Post* presented a chart depicting the Christian school explosion:

Christian Schools in the United States

Year	Schools
1965	1,000
1970-71	2,500
1980-81	7,500
1984-85	*13,000

Projected

Although 13,000 Christian schools had been projected by the conclusion of the 1984-85 school year, that projection turned out to be quite low. Paul A. Kienel, president of ACSI, reports that a curriculum publisher conducted a search in the Library of Congress and could account for more than *32,000* Christian schools! The increase in enrollment among Christian schools continued until 1987 at which time it began to decrease.

Notice the correlation: when the number of students in private/religious schools began increasing, the scores began to improve from their dramatic slide; when the number of students attending private/religious schools began to decline, so did the scores. While this correlation is of interest, students in private/religious schools could have caused a positive impact on the scores only if they achieve higher SAT scores than their counterparts in public schools.

In 1987, the College Board began to separate the SAT scores in a manner which allows comparison of scores between students from private/religious schools and their peers in public schools. The results are shown on the graph below:

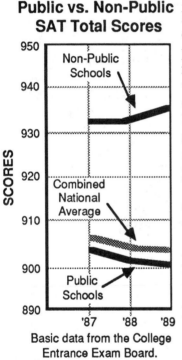

Public vs. Non-Public SAT Total Scores

Basic data from the College Entrance Exam Board.

Since public school scores are lower than the national totals, it is evident that were it not for the positive effect of the private/religious scores, the SAT scores would be even lower than they currently are. The disparity between public and non-public scores since 1987 is great enough to suggest that the same differences probably existed prior to 1987.

Furthermore, in the years of decreasing private/religious school enrollment—the years when the SAT again turned downward—the private/religious school scores were improving. For the national scores to be declining when private/religious school scores are improving shows that there simply are no longer enough private school students to pull the national totals upward against the much greater pressure of the public school students who are pulling the scores downward.

A further indicator of superior Christian school achievement is provided through the Stanford Achievement Test, an achievement test used in both public and private schools nationally. The Association of Christian Schools International (ACSI), comprised of 2,700 affiliate schools and 475,000 students, utilizes this test. Notice the difference between Christian school and public school scores on the same test:

Public School vs. ACSI Christian School
Stanford Achievement Scores

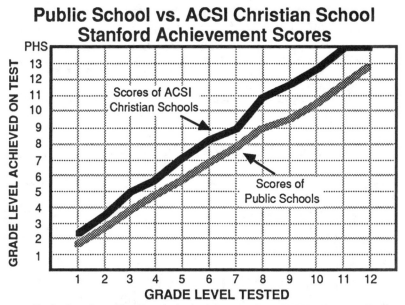

Basic data from The Psychological Corporation, 1988 testing results.

Another academic test which shows comparable disparities in favor of private/religious school students is the PSAT-NMSQT (Preliminary Scholastic Aptitude Test - National Merit Scholarship Qualifying Test). High scores on this test can qualify a student to receive National Merit Scholarships. Those who qualify as semi-finalists for the Scholarships are considered the academic "cream of the crop"—the top 1/2 percentile of their state's graduating class. In the 1988 results, only 15,414 students qualified as semi-finalists from the initial field of 1,213,042 students originally tested. Following the release of the 1988 results, a survey was undertaken to determine which schools were the source of these academically superior students.

According to the Department of Education, at the time of the testing, 87.6 percent of the students attended public schools and 12.4 percent attended private/religious schools. With public schools having 87.6 percent of the students, they would be expected to produce 87.6 percent of the semi-finalists; 12.4 percent of the semi-finalists would be expected from private/

religious schools. Surprisingly, the survey revealed that 39.2 percent of the stellar academic performers came from private/ religious schools—a percentage three times greater than their proportional size! (The detailed results of that survey are provided in Appendix C).

The following graph indicates the disproportionately positive impact of private schools:

Student Population vs. Achievement

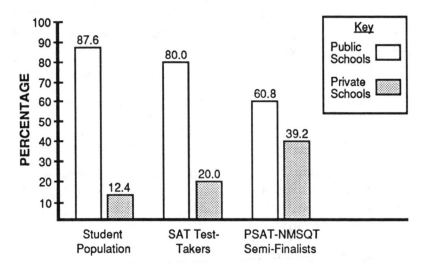

With private schools proportionally...

...supplying 1.6 times more SAT-takers than their relative percentage (20 percent as opposed to 12.4 percent),

...supplying 3.2 times more than their relative percentage of academically elite students (39.2 percent as opposed to 12.4 percent),

...producing students with higher achievement scores than their public school counterparts at all grade levels,

private schools are having a positive academic effect dramatically greater than their relative size.

Some have tried to dismiss the stark difference in academic achievements between private and public schools by arguing that affluency is the major reason that private schools surpass public schools in academic achievements. However, when the money expended per student in private schools (an indicator of affluency) is compared with public schools, it is apparent that money is not a significant factor in private school achievement:

School Expenditures--Public vs. Private

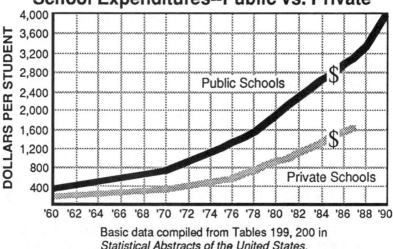

Basic data compiled from Tables 199, 200 in
Statistical Abstracts of the United States.

Private schools are spending only half the money per student as public schools, yet have higher achievement! Additionally, in 1984, the median income of those sending their children to private schools was $26,500, only slightly higher than the national median. However, the slightly higher income of private school families actually doesn't exist since private school families pay for their children's education twice: they pay public school taxes and private school tuitions/fees. When the average tuition cost of only _one_ student (the average family includes two children) is deducted from the average income of private-school families, *public school families actually have _more_ unrestricted money* available for their children than do those who send their children to private school.

In the consideration of enhanced private/religious school achievements, an observation should be made: the primary difference between private/religious schools and public schools is not in the core curriculum. The Civil War occurs the same years at both types of schools; math tables remain the same; and a verb does not become an adjective merely because a student attends a religious school. Since the core academic curriculum— the basis for educational testing—is fundamentally the same for both types of schools, there is reason to believe that the measurable differences in academic achievement may be attributed to the educational philosophy under which the curriculum is applied. In 72 percent of private schools, religious principles hold a prominent position in the school's educational philosophy and instructional process.

Conflicting Academic Standards

Even though students' achievement test scores have fallen dramatically since 1962-63, their report card scores have actually risen! The top graph reflects students' report card grades (collected and released by the American College Testing Program, the producers of the ACT test). By examining only report card scores (the top graph), one could easily conclude that students were showing academic improvement—afterall, their report card scores are *rising* year after year. However, the bottom chart reveals that student achievement as measured on the ACT test (a college-bound test similar to the SAT) has been *declining* during the same time. Students have actually been receiving higher marks in school for knowing less—a clear contradiction in educational standards!

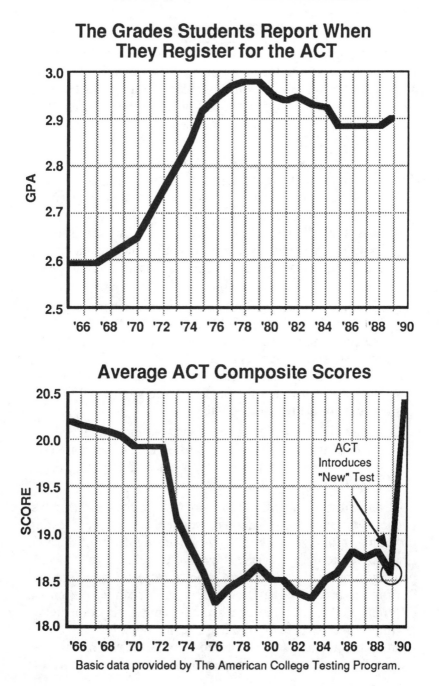

The Grades Students Report When They Register for the ACT

Average ACT Composite Scores

Basic data provided by The American College Testing Program.

(Teacher Competency Testing)

With the growing awareness of poor student performance, attention has begun to focus not only on the educational system in general, but on teachers in particular. Features such as the *Dallas Times Herald* special report of December 11-21, 1983, can be found in most major newspapers across the country. Notice these highlights:

- Twenty states have acted to stem the flow of teachers who can't spell, add or punctuate by requiring competency testing for teachers. When the test was given last April to 1,269 juniors in Texas teacher education programs, 38 percent failed the exam, which tests basic skills taught by the 12th grade, such as calculating percentages, capitalizing words and comprehending a 200-word passage.

- The test was also given to 3,300 new teachers in the Houston Independent School District. Because of cheating and other irregularities, scores for only 2,400 of the teachers were reported. Almost two-thirds—62 percent—failed the exam. The Houston School Board later lowered the passing score so that only 44 percent of the teachers failed.

- Dallas school officials say that, on the same test, 1,223 of the 2,280 teachers hired by the Dallas school district since 1979 (54%) could not correctly answer 67 percent of the questions.

In an effort to weed out the most incompetent teachers, twenty-six states have adopted teacher competency testing programs, although only twenty-two currently publish their results. While many observers believe that the teacher incompetency problem is not severe, *What's Happening in Teacher Testing,* prepared by the Department of Education, presents a different picture. In the states publicizing their competency testing results, 17 percent of the applicants failed!

Since the average score required to pass the exam was only around 50 percent, it is a very generous statement to report that only 17 percent of the applicants are unqualified. Had the passing mark been raised above 50 percent, the percentage of "unqualified" or "incompetent" teachers would have risen significantly.

Since the Bible teaches that "a student will become like his teacher" (Luke 6:40), it is appropriate to be concerned about teacher competency. Nearly 41,000,000 students were enrolled in public schools in 1990; if 17 percent of the students were taught by incompetent teachers, that translates to 7 million adversely affected students. The Biblical admonition that "the student will become like his teacher" is sobering. Can we afford for 7 million students to become like their teachers?

According to statistics made available during a White House briefing attended by the author in September 1989, 700,000 students *graduated* from high school in June 1986 who were unable to read their own diplomas after completing 12 years of formal education! The thought of releasing so many academically crippled students to take their place in the community, in business, and in the nation is frightening.

The weakening academic abilities of students has resulted in a 72 percent increase in the number of colleges and universities adding remedial courses to accommodate the lower skills levels of their entrants.[8] Such a lowering of the course content will produce weaker degree programs, which will result in weaker college graduates, many of whom will re-enter the educational arena as teachers. This process is, in fact, what is occurring: since 1973, the SAT scores of prospective teachers have fallen 55 points,[9] and the Department of Education reports "half of the newly qualified mathematics, science, and English teachers are not qualified to teach these subjects."[10] Weaker teachers in turn produce weaker students, that in turn produce weaker degree programs in colleges and universities, that in turn produce weaker teachers, that in turn.... To reproduce this scenario on a continuing basis is unacceptable, yet this is what is currently happening.

(Dropouts)

In addition to declining academic achievement and increasing teacher incompetency, there is an alarmingly high dropout rate.[11] The General Educational Development test—a high-school equivalency test available since 1918 for those who did not graduate from high school—indicates the magnitude of the problem.

School Dropouts And G.E.D. Testing

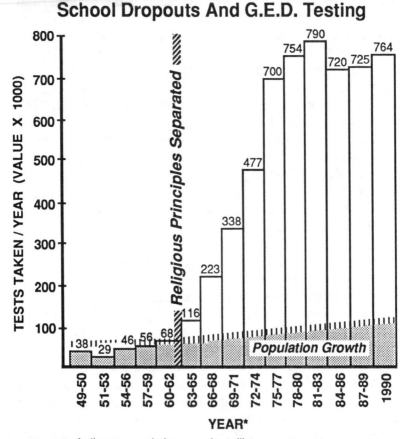

IIIIIIIIIIIII Indicates population growth profile.

* Groupings represent average tests taken per year for the 3-year period.

Basic data from the General Educational Development Testing Service of The American Council on Education and the Department of Commerce, Census Bureau.

A New Class of Problems

For years, the standards for behavior and for right and wrong were derived largely from religious teachings. When those teachings were disallowed in 1962, they were replaced with value-free teachings, allowing students to "discover" and set their own standards—the results are evident.

Lack of discipline and school violence are now the more troublesome problems facing America's schools. Fourteen of the fifteen Gallup polls on schools during 1968-1983 cited lack of discipline as the primary problem. Before the ban on religious teachings in education, the top public school offenses were listed as: [12]

1. Talking
2. Chewing gum
3. Making noise
4. Running in the halls
5. Getting out of turn in line
6. Wearing improper clothing
7. Not putting paper in wastebaskets

Polls now list the top public schools offenses as: [13]

1. Rape
2. Robbery
3. Assault
4. Burglary
5. Arson
6. Bombings
7. Murder
8. Suicide
9. Absenteeism
10. Vandalism
11. Extortion
12. Drug abuse
13. Alcohol abuse
14. Gang warfare
15. Pregnancies
16. Abortions
17. Venereal disease

School Violence

To suggest that violence in public schools has now become a significant problem is a mammoth understatement. News articles such as this one from the December 8, 1986, *Los Angeles Times* have become commonplace across the nation:

At most of the Oakland Unified School District's 92 schools, the fight against crime and violence is unending. An Uzi semiautomatic rifle, with 15 hollow-point bullets, was among the weapons confiscated by district officials within the last year.

Franklin *Elementary School*...trying to ensure that students know to hit the ground when bullets fly, *carries out "shooting" drills twice a year.*

From the May 22, 1988, *Fort Worth Star-Telegram:*

School officials learned about the most recent [sexual] assault Friday after investigators talked to the 11-year old victim. The sixth-grade student...was assaulted on two occasions at school while she waited for her parents to pick her up.

The girl told investigators that two 13-year-old boys raped her in a girls' restroom at school two weeks ago. On Thursday, one of the same boys and three of his friends returned to where she again was waiting. The girl told police the boys took her back into the school against her will, and two of them raped her behind a stairwell while the other two watched, according to a police report.

A 15-year-old girl told police she was [sexually] assaulted May 10 in an empty ROTC room...She named an 18-year-old student as her attacker.

Another assault reportedly occurred May 11 behind a stage curtain in a...school auditorium. The 16-year-old victim told police she was held by two students while a third raped her.

The April 29, 1987, *New York Times* carried this feature on Detroit schools:

On the average, a child was shot every day in 1986...The city canceled classes Monday and today to hold assemblies on youth violence.

Just before spring break...a 14-year-old student firing a .357 magnum pistol chased a star football player through the halls of Murray-Wright High School...as others looked on helpless and in horror. The football player was killed by a bullet to the head. Two other students were wounded. Parents are demanding metal detectors and searches for weapons in the schools.

The call for [weapons] searches has reignited a debate that raged a few years ago, when officials conducted random searches for a time but stopped after the American Civil Liberties Union sued in 1985...

City officials said they would resume weapons searches in the schools. *"I'm tired of kids carrying guns like they used to take a lunch,"* Mayor Coleman Young said.

The January 16, 1991, *Chicago Sun-Times* reported:

A new security program that brought 150 police officers into the Chicago public schools resulted in an unprecedented 4,306 arrests in the first four months of this school year...

Police made nearly 14 times the number of drug arrests as had been made in the previous fall and nearly 12 times the weapons arrests...

There were 1,122 arrests for disorderly conduct...910 for battery and 738 for criminal trespass...229 [for] alleged weapons violations...

"I'm proud of the fact we're taking action to reduce the level of violence in the schools" [said George H. Sams, head of security for Chicago's 600 public schools].

The December 13, 1985, *National Review* reported:

- In New York City in the first four months of the 1984-85 academic year, school security officers, using *spot checks,* were able to confiscate one thousand *weapons.*

- In 1984, 120 students were shot in Detroit schools.

- During a five-month period in 1981, one-hundred-thousand incidents of violence were reported in California schools.

The 1978 "Safe Schools Study" by the National Institute of Education reported:

- The risk of violence to teenagers is greater in public schools than elsewhere.

- Only 17 to 19 percent of violent offenses against urban youths 12 to 15 occur in the street. Sixty-eight percent of the robberies and 50 percent of the assaults on youngsters of this age occur at school.

- An estimated 282,000 secondary school students reported that they were attacked *at school* in a typical *one-month period.*

Information from the National School Safety Center shows that in 1982-83, Boston's Safe Schools Commission found:

- Nearly 4 out of 10 students were often fearful for their safety in school or reported avoiding certain locations like corridors and restrooms.

- 3 out of 10 students admitted carrying weapons to school.

- Half of the teachers and 40 percent of the students had been victims of school robbery, assault or larceny.

Additionally: [14]

- 5,200 high-school teachers were physically attacked each month, with one-fifth requiring medical treatment.

- Attacks on teachers are five times more likely to result in serious injury than attacks on students.

- Only one in three offenses committed on school campuses are reported to school officials.

An article in the September 9, 1990, *Fort Worth Star Telegram* revealed the current trend in student "fashions":

Bulletproof back-to-school clothes are the latest thing for...children who run a dangerous gantlet to and from class. School blazers and other jackets fitted with bullet-resistant Kevlar 129 pads...Added shielding from flying bullets can be had from a bulletproof book bag or clipboard. They're offered by [a] former New York City police officer.

(*Student Suicides*)

Not only have students become violent in their interpersonal confrontations; they have become violent toward themselves. Suicides among youth 15-24 have increased 253 percent since the separation of religious principles (an average increase of 10.5 percent per year).[15] *Minimum* estimates indicate that 400,000 adolescents attempt suicide each year—one every 80 seconds[16]—and many estimates place the attempts at nearly 2,000,000 per year—one every 15 seconds. In 1962, suicide ranked 12th in the cause of death among young people; in 1987, it ranked 2nd.[17]

(*Basic Subject Knowledge Lacking*)

An environment where violence, disrespect, and immorality prevails is not conducive to learning. There have been such declines in students' knowledge of basic academic facts that on March 17, 1986, U.S. Senator Bill Bradley moved to designate a "Geography Awareness Week." A survey taken in January of that year which had examined five-thousand high-school *seniors* from eight major cities on their knowledge of basic geography had precipitated his move. The results?

- 25 percent of the students tested in Dallas could not identify the country that borders the United States on the south.

- 39 percent of the students in Boston could not name the six New England states.

- 45 percent of those tested in Baltimore could not respond correctly to this instruction: "On the attached map, shade in the area where the United States is located."

Similar geographic weaknesses were discovered in a survey of *college* students conducted by the University of North Carolina in 1984:

- When asked to identify the two largest states, fewer than half of them could name Texas and Alaska.

- Almost 80 percent couldn't name the two smallest states.

Bradley concluded: "This news...is frightening. We depend on a well-informed populace to maintain the democratic ideals which have made our country great. When 95 percent of some of our *brightest* college students cannot locate Vietnam on a world map, we must sound the alarm. We cannot expect to be a world leader if our populace doesn't even know who the rest of the world is!"

Basic historical knowledge appears to be at the same substandard level as basic geographical knowledge. A 1988 Department of Education book entitled *American Education: Making It Work* concluded: "Many students are unaware of prominent people and seminal ideas and events that have shaped our past and created our present." That statement resulted from a 1986 assessment of 17 year-old students, 80 percent of whom were enrolled in U.S. History classes at the time of the testing. What were some of the problem areas?

- Almost half could not place World War I between 1900 and 1950.

- More than two-thirds did not know when the Civil War took place.

- More than 75 percent were unable to say within 20 years when Abraham Lincoln was President.

- One-fifth of the students could not identify George Washington as the commander of the Colonial forces during the Revolution.

- One-third did not know that Lincoln was the author of the Emancipation Proclamation.

- One-half failed to recognize Patrick Henry as the man who said, "Give me liberty or give me death!"

- One-third did not know that the Declaration of Independence signaled the American Colonists' break from England.

- Almost half could not say even approximately when the Constitution was written.

International Testing

American academic weaknesses become even more glaring when American students are compared with their peers in other nations. In 1983, the *Dallas Times Herald* asked four educational experts to develop a test covering math, science, and geography which was given to 12-year old students in eight nations. The results of that international testing are shown on the following page; the United States did very poorly.

International Testing
Percentage of Correct Answers

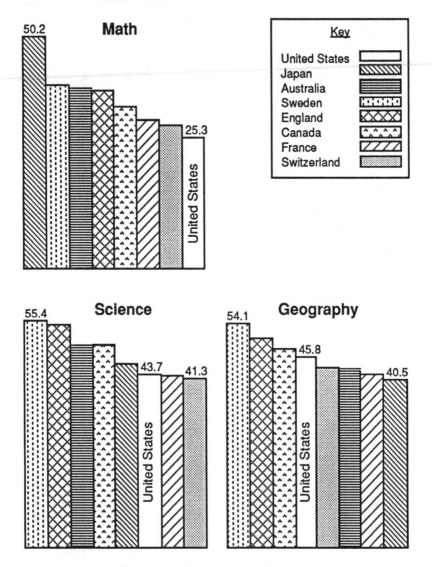

Basic data from "American Education: The ABCs of Failure,"
Dallas Times Herald, December 11-21, 1983.

For decades, the U.S. has participated in academic competition against other nations, but never before with these results:

- International comparisons of student achievement reveal that on 19 academic tests, American students were *never* first or second and, in comparison with other industrialized nations, were *last* seven times. [18]

- In a test comparing average American public school sixth-graders with their counterparts in seven other Western industrialized countries, American public school students ranked *last* in mathematics and not much better in science and geography. [19]

- Our 14-year-old science students placed 14th—tied with Singapore and Thailand—out of 17 competing countries. Advanced American science students fare even more poorly: 9th of 13 countries in physics, 11th of 13 in chemistry, and *last* in biology. [20]

- In a 1982 testing of 12th grade students among 11 nations, the United States placed *last* in algebra, and was ahead of only Hungary in calculus. When considering only the brightest students—the top five percent of each category—the United States was *last* in both algebra and calculus. [21]

- In a 1988 international assessment of math and science among six developed countries, American students ranked *last* in mathematics and next to last overall in science. [22]

The poor performance of American students on international math competitions, particularly after scoring so highly in previous decades, prompted further investigation into the math abilities of American students. The December 11-21, 1983, *Dallas Times Herald* special edition reported some of the findings:

- A University of Michigan study of math achievement among fifth-graders found that the highest-achieving American class did worse than the lowest-performing

Japanese class. Only one of the 100 top-scoring students was an American.

- A University of Illinois at Chicago study found that the average American high school student would rank 99th in math when compared with 100 average Japanese students.

(Trans-National Studies)

While other nations have remained the same or even improved academically, America's educational system has been on a downward spiral and holds neither a superior status nor a good reputation in the eyes of the international community. Perhaps the lack of respect toward the American educational system is best illustrated by the results of a two-year cooperative study conducted between Japan and the United States in 1985-1986. Teams of scholars from each nation made extensive visits to the other's schools to identify ingredients which would be helpful for their own educational system.

In January 1987, the Department of Education released the results of their two-year study in a report titled *Japanese Education Today* with an epilogue titled *Implications for American Education*. These reports specifically identified numerous aspects of the Japanese system that the experts felt should be incorporated into the American system.*

Japanese officials released their six-page report at the same time, but with significantly differing conclusions. After two

---

* The conclusion of the American investigators is ironic: the current Japanese educational system is actually the American educational system of the late 1940's which was placed in Japan by the United States as part of reconstruction after World War II! Members of General Douglas MacArthur's staff who participated in building Japan's system in the 40's and 50's have commented that the successful elements of the Japanese system have changed little since the time of their implementation in the late 40's. Therefore, the contrasts between Japan's current educational successes and our failures become even more painful when realizing that Japan's present system is built on the American educational system of four decades ago!

years of study, they found *no specific aspect of American education that they considered worth emulating!* As reported in the January 8, 1987, *New York Times:*

> "It is not our intention that contents of the current American educational system...be proposed as elements of educational reform in Japan," the study said. "Recently, the outcome of common math tests show Japanese kids scoring higher than Americans," said Mr. Amagi, who led the study for the Ministry of Education. "American scholars," Mr. Amagi went on, "seem to share the view that the American educational system has fallen into mediocrity.   American kids register very bad scores on international tests." Quoting from recent studies by American educators, the Japanese researchers cited the worries in the United States about teacher skills, dropout rates, poor student performance and lowered college standards.

It is a potent commentary on the current state of American education when, after two years of extensive study, the Japanese researchers could find *"no* specific aspect of American education...considered worth emulating."

(*American Education and Business*)

The academic decline in America's public schools has posed a threat to the business community. American business has restructured many programs in order to accommodate weaker students; the reason for that restructuring is obvious:

- In [1987], New York Telephone Co. gave its simple 50-minute exam in basic reading and reasoning skills to 21,000 applicants for entry-level jobs. Only 16 percent passed. [23]

- A Department of Education study found that one in three young adults with a degree from a two- or four-year college could not correctly answer this question: "If you spend $1.95 for a sandwich and 60 cents for a bowl of soup, and give the cashier $3, how much change should you receive?" The answer is 45 cents, but one-third of the college graduates missed it. [24]

- A University of Texas study revealed that of 15,000 people tested, forty percent could not figure correct change from a store purchase.

- In 1987, a number of banks in the New York City public school district agreed to place some 400 students into entry level positions. The bank's criterion for employment was nothing more than simple, standard job entry skills, but they were able to qualify only 100 students. The others did not even have the basic reading and writing skills required for employment.

Since businesses can no longer assume that their employees have received sufficient training in fundamental academic skills, many corporations are setting aside significant portions of their annual budget for remedial education for their employees. In an article in the *Los Angeles Times,* David T. Kearns, Chief Executive Officer of the Xerox Corporation, stated:

American business will have to hire more than a million new service and production workers a year who can't read, write or count. Teaching them how, and absorbing the lost productivity while they are learning, will cost industry $25 billion a year, and nobody seems to know how long such remedial training will be necessary.

Three out of four major corporations already are giving new workers basic reading, writing and arithmetic courses...*Corporate training is bigger than our entire elementary, secondary and higher education system put together...*

It is a terrible admission, but $25 billion a year for remedial training has become a necessary added cost of doing business.

The special report of the December 11-21, 1983, *Dallas Times Herald* reported:

While working for Chrysler Corp., John C. Graves found in 1980 that the majority of new assembly line workers hired (most of them recent high-school graduates) could read at only a sixth-grade level and do only fourth-grade math.

He blames the curriculum and promotion policies of schools: "These people should never have gotten out of school in the first place."

Now training and development manager at a Rockwell International plant that makes nuclear devices in Colorado, Graves finds that nearly all new assembly line employees need basic skills training before they can learn their jobs.

Employees must read and compute at a seventh- to ninth-grade level to be trainable at his plant, Graves said. "We're finding that a majority of people are not coming into the work place with skills that high."

The September 28, 1987, *Wall Street Journal* reported:

Motorola feels it must supplement the skills of entry-level workers who "have nowhere near the mathematical competence of our Japanese competitors," says Edward W. Bales, director of operations...Mr. Bales cites a recent study by the federally funded International Association for the Evaluation of Education Achievement, which found, among other things, that *elementary-school pupils in Japan had reached the same level of math competence as junior-high-school students in the U.S.*

It is ironic in the fact of these deficiencies that schools claim their students are prepared to enter the work force:

A report published in 1983 by the Center for Public Resources...[found that] while most companies reported basic skills deficiencies in most job categories, over 75 percent of the school system rated their graduates as "academically prepared" in the basic academic skills needed for employment. [25]

American Education and the Armed Forces

Not only are many high school graduates not academically prepared for business, many are unable to qualify at military minimums for the Armed Forces. The July 8, 1986, *New York Times* reported on the academic problems of Navy recruits:

A...study of naval personnel, authorized last year by Admiral Watkins, recently retired Chief of Naval Operations...found that more than 20 percent of... recruits in 1983 and 1984 were unable to read at the ninth-grade level, the minimum level required for dealing with technical manuals that are essential to their training and job skills. Yet...88.5 percent of the sample of 67,686 individuals had high school diplomas.

He added that 97 percent of those who could not make it through boot camp—mainly because of their flawed knowledge of reading—had high school diplomas...

The Navy...has had to spend $25 million a year for *remedial* reading programs...and drug and alcohol abuse prevention and rehabilitation.

Of the 1.9 million young men who now enter the labor force each year...about 600,000 are unfit for military service without extensive remedial training... "We know from experience that, of that 600,000, we can remediate at least half," he said. "Why aren't they remediated ahead of time?"

Information on the educational problems of many Air Force and Army recruits was provided in a special report of the December 11-21, 1983, *Dallas Times Herald:*

Three years ago [1980], 54 percent of the 18-year-olds in the United States were qualified to enter the Air Force; today that has dropped to 34 percent...Although 98 percent of the recruits now have high school diplomas, the Air Force still finds itself with people who can't read at the ninth-grade level, which is necessary to complete training.

The number of Army recruits whose reading and math abilities are below the ninth-grade level increased sharply during the past decade. In 1975 only 10 percent of the recruits fell into that category, but 45 percent of the 1981 recruits could not read or do math as well as average ninth-graders...Since 1979, the Army has spent more than $160 million...to provide remedial education for recruits.

An Overview of American Education

The Department of Education released an assessment of the overall condition of American schools in its report *A Nation At Risk*. Highlights from that report are listed below:

- For the first time in the history of our country, the educational skills of one generation will not surpass, will not equal, will not even approach, those of their parents.

- Thirty-five states require only 1 year of mathematics, and 36 require only 1 year of science for a high-school diploma.

- A study of the typical public school schedule found that the average school provided only 22 hours of academic instruction during the week.

- In 13 states, 50 percent or more of the units required for high school graduation may be electives chosen by the student. Given this freedom to choose the substance of half or more of their education, many students opt for less demanding personal service courses, such as bachelor living.

- In many schools, the time spent learning how to cook and drive counts as much toward a high school diploma as the time spent studying mathematics, English, chemistry, American history, or biology.

- Nearly 40 percent of 17 year-olds cannot draw inferences from written material, and only a third can solve a math problem requiring several steps.

- A recent study revealed that a majority of students were able to master 80 percent of the material in some of their texts before they had even opened the books.

Since 1962-63, numerous attempts have been made to reverse the academic deterioration: improving the student/teacher ratio; increasing teacher salaries; elevated spending on public education, etc. (For more information on the statistical results of these efforts, see the author's book *What Happened In Education?*) Despite these efforts, the quality of education has continued to decline. Ben Franklin's rebuff to the Constitutional Convention's delegates after days of fruitless endeavors in the early part of the Convention seems appropriate here:

> In this situation...how has it happened, Sir, that we have not hitherto once thought of humbly applying to the Father of lights...*Have we now forgotten this powerful Friend? Or do we imagine we no longer need His assistance?*...We have been assured, Sir, in the Sacred Writings that except the Lord build the house, they labor in vain that build it. I firmly believe this; and I also believe that without His concurring aid, we shall succeed...no better than the builders of Babel. [26]

Extensive effort has been expended on our public educational system over recent decades, all without asking any aid of God. Measurements indicate that, to a large part, those labors have been in vain. However, substantially higher achievements are recorded by those schools who never separated God and His principles from their academic endeavors.

Except the Lord build the house... (Psalms 127:1)

Chapter 5
"Our Country"—The Nation

In national policy—just as with each previous category—
prior to 1962, the Courts had consistently ruled that Christian
principles were vital to and must be included in public policy.
They stressed that Christianity was part of the common law
(i.e., the foundation on which all other laws rested):

> This wise legislature framed this great body of laws for
> a Christian country and Christian people...This is the
> Christianity of the common law....in this the
> Constitution of the United States has made no altera-
> tion....No free government now exists in the world
> unless where Christianity is acknowledged, and is the
> religion of the country...it is the...only stable support of
> all human laws. [1] *Updegraph v. Commonwealth*

> Christianity is part of the common law of the land...It has
> always been so recognized...The U.S. Constitution
> allows it as a part of the common law....In the Courts over
> which we preside, we daily acknowledge Christianity as
> the most solemn part of our administration. A...witness...
> [places] his hand upon...the books of the New Testament,
> which testify of our Savior's birth, life, death, and resur-
> rection; this is so common a matter, that it is little thought
> of as an evidence of the part which Christianity has in the
> common law. [2] *Charleston v. S. A. Benjamin*

> Whatever strikes at the root of Christianity tends
> manifestly to the dissolution of civil government...
> because it tends to corrupt the morals of the people, and
> to destroy good order. [3] *People v. Ruggles*

Despite scores of cases with similar declarations, in 1962-63
the Court declared exactly the opposite The rulings since 1962-
63 have encouraged indiscriminate warfare against traditional
religious principles. In 1961, there were very few serious
challenges against religious principles in public affairs; by the
mid-70s, there were eighty-four cases;[4] however, from 1980-

1991 the number had soared to *over 3,000 legal challenges!* [5] The Court's message was clear: Christian religious expressions are not welcome in public affairs and will be taken to Court. This policy, judged by the warnings and predictions of the Founders, is a blueprint for a domestic disaster. Notice George Washington's warning in his Farewell Address:

> Of all the dispositions and habits which lead to political prosperity, religion and morality are indispensable supports. In vain would that man claim the tribute of patriotism, who should labour to subvert [religion and morality]...The mere politician, equally with the pious man, ought to respect and to cherish them...Where is the security for property, for reputation, for life, [without] the sense of religious obligation?...Who that is a sincere friend to it can look with indifference upon attempts to shake the foundation of this fabric? [6]

Powerful words from the Father of the Country: do not let anyone claim to be a true patriot if he attempts to subvert religion and morality from politics! Noah Webster, another Founder, articulated the belief cherished by the Framers of the Constitution:

> The moral principles and precepts contained in the Scriptures ought to form the basis of all our civil consti-tutions and laws...*All the miseries and evils which men suffer from vice, crime, ambition, injustice, oppres-sion, slavery, and war, proceed from their despising or neglecting the precepts contained in the Bible.* [7]

A very wise insight: most problems are the result of ignoring or improperly applying God's Word. Webster's warning, coupled with Washington's warning ("Where is the security for property, for reputation, for life, [without] the sense of religious obliga-tion?")[8] form an incredibly accurate prediction of what occurred in the nation. The following graph indicates the loss of security for both property and life which has occurred since the Court "despis[ed] or neglect[ed] the precepts found in the Bible."

Violent Crime: Number Of Offenses

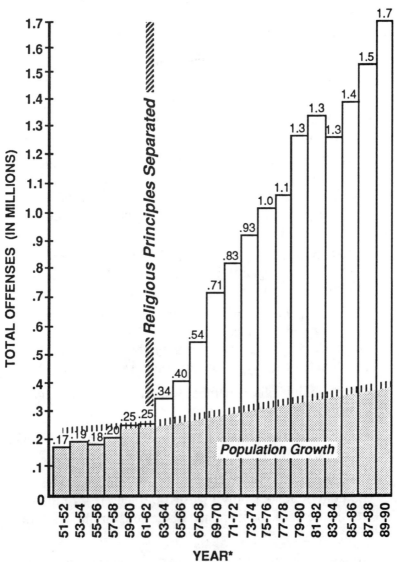

IIIIIIIIII Indicates population growth profile.

* Groupings represent average rate per year over the two-year period.

Basic data from *Statistical Abstracts of the United States,*
and the Department of Commerce, Census Bureau.

(Information on Crime)

Since religious principles were excluded from public affairs in 1962, crime has exploded:

- Between 1960 and 1980, the number of serious crimes (murders, rapes, robberies, burglaries) increased 332 percent. [9]

- 57 million Americans—one in four—are annual victims of crime. [10]

- Crime costs U.S. citizens a total of $300 billion annually—an amount equal to almost 40 percent of the U.S. budget. If returned, that money could bring a windfall of $1,250 to every man, woman, and child in the country. [11]

- $10.6 billion was stolen from individual citizens in 1981; crimes against businesses cost at least $39.7 billion. [12]

- U.S. companies spend more than $4 billion a year for security and still lose more than $7 billion a year to shoplifters. Stores raise their prices as much as 15 percent to cover losses due to crime. [13]

- Many individuals remember when it was safe enough to go to sleep with their back doors unlocked.

Thomas Jefferson explained why civil government cannot control crime apart from Christian principles:

> The precepts of philosophy, and of the [old legal] code, laid hold of actions only. [Jesus] pushed his scrutinies into the heart of man, erected his tribunal in the region of his thoughts. [14]

Civil laws cannot deal with the heart, which is the actual seat of violence, crime, drug abuse, immorality, etc. Only religious principles can stop a crime *before* it occurs, because only religious principles can control the heart. For example, religion can deal with murder *before* it occurs—while it is still only a thought in the heart; civil and criminal laws can do nothing until after the fact. Understanding this principle, the Founders refused to allow the separation of religious principles from government:

> We have no government armed with power capable of contending with human passions unbridled by morality and religion. Avarice, ambition, revenge or gallantry would break the strongest cords of our Constitution as a whale goes through a net. Our Constitution was made only for a moral and religious people. It is wholly inadequate to the government of any other. [15] JOHN ADAMS

> We have staked the whole future of American civilization, not upon the power of government, far from it. We have staked the future of all our political institutions...upon the capacity of each and all of us to govern ourselves, to control ourselves, to sustain ourselves according to the Ten Commandments of God. [16] JAMES MADISON

> The cultivation of the religious sentiment...inspires respect for law and order and gives strength to the whole social fabric. [17] DANIEL WEBSTER

The Courts have now set aside the sagacity and foresight of the Founders.

National Productivity

In the education section, it was demonstrated that the absence of religious principles (from which teachings on self-control, respect, honesty, hard-work, etc. are derived) created an environment leading to sub-standard achievement and an inferior work-ethic. Since students carry their educational training and work-ethic into the work place with them, it is not surprising that business is similarly affected. The following two graphs demonstrate this vividly:

Multi-Factor Productivity:
Non-Farm Business

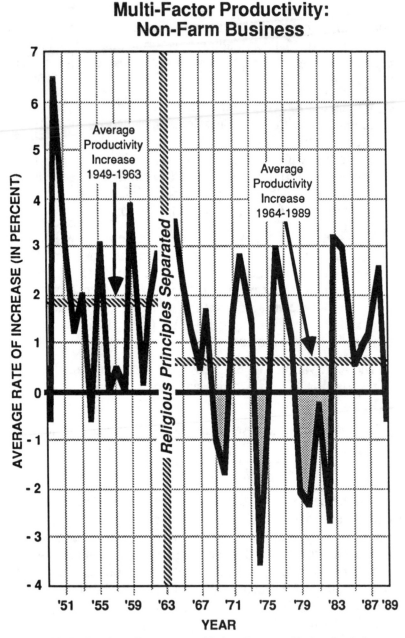

Basic data from Department of Labor, Bureau of Labor Statistics.

Multi-Factor Productivity: Private Business

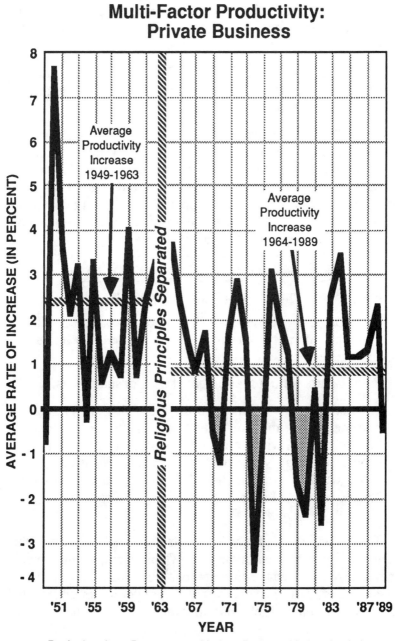

Basic data from Department of Labor, Bureau of Labor Statistics.

A Department of Labor study comparing productivity among 12 manufacturing countries (the United States, Canada, Japan, France, Germany, Italy, United Kingdom, Belgium, Denmark, Netherlands, Norway and Sweden) revealed:

> Since 1960...the United States shows the largest productivity decline. [18]

The effect of the persistent decline in productivity on the U.S. economy is substantial. Had the pre-1962 productivity rate continued, output in 1979 would have been 12 percent higher than it was, *without any additional capital or labor used in production!* That additional 12 percent output is much larger than that needed to solve many of today's economic problems, most notably the budget deficit! [19]

Sexually Transmitted Diseases (STDs)

Recall Washington's warning about morality:

> Reason and experience both forbid us to expect that national morality can prevail in exclusion of religious principles. [20]

Early Courts were just as poignant in their statements:

> Christianity has reference to the principles of right and wrong...it is the foundation of those morals and manners upon which our society is formed....The day of moral virtue in which we live would, in an instant, if that standard were abolished, lapse into the dark and murky night of Pagan immorality. [21] *City of Charleston v. S. A. Benjamin*

The Founders and early Courts believed fervently that Christianity produced morality. Consequently, they would never have tolerated the current separation. Notice how accurate the Founders and Courts were in their predictions of what would happen to morality if religious principles were separated:

Cases Of Sexually Transmitted Diseases

Includes: Gonorrhea, Syphilis, Chancroid, Granuloma
Inguinale, Lymphogranuloma Venereum, and AIDS

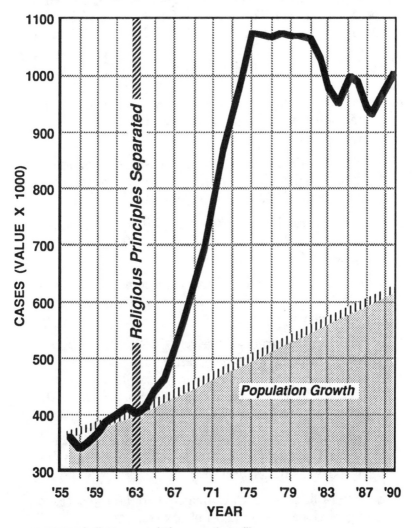

IIIIIIIIIII Indicates population growth profile.

Basic data from Department of Health and Human Services, the Center
for Disease Control, and the Department of Commerce, Census Bureau.

The loss of national morality has resulted in a national outbreak of sexually-transmitted diseases. The current STD epidemic (there are now more than 25 different types of sexually-transmitted diseases!) infects an average of *33,000 people a day!* At this rate, 1 in 4 Americans between the ages of 15 and 55 eventually will acquire an STD. [22] In 1986 alone, there were 15,000 *new* cases of AIDS, 90,000 *new* cases of syphilis, 500,000 *new* cases of genital herpes, 1,000,000 *new* cases of venereal warts, 1,800,000 *new* cases of gonorrhea, 3,000,000 *new* cases of trichomaniasis, 3,000,000 *new* cases of chlamydia, and 2,450,000 *new* cases of other STDs, representing a total of nearly *12 million new cases.* [23]

- Between 1965 and 1975, the cases of gonorrhea tripled[24] and in 1984 alone there were 2 million cases of gonorrhea and 90,000 cases of syphilis. [25]

- Between 1966 and 1984, genital herpes *increased 1,500 percent* [26] and now infects 500,000 *new victims annually.* [27]

- Between 1966 and 1983, molluscum contagiosum (which causes lesions in the genital area) *increased 1,100 percent.* [28]

- Pelvic inflammatory disease (PID), causes over 210,000 women to be *hospitalized* annually, many of whom are being involuntarily sterilized by the disease. In 1976, nearly 80,000 women were made sterile by gonococcal PID. [29]

- Chlamydia trachomatis—the fastest-growing STD—infects *3 to 4 million annually* and causes sterility in 11,000 women each year. [30]

- In 1984 there were an estimated 1 million *new* cases of genital warts—an STD linked to cancer. [31]

- STDs now cost more than *$2 billion annually* in health-care. [32]

The effects of STDs are not limited solely to those involved in promiscuous sexual relations; STDs in pregnant women affect the fetus and the newborn:

- Chlamydia causes lung and eye infections in newborns. [33]

- Neonatal herpes frequently causes death or permanent neurological damage to the newborn. [34]

- Venereal warts, transmitted to an infant during delivery, lodge in the larynx, trachea and lungs. [35]

In addition to the physical consequences, there can be serious emotional and psychological effects associated with STDs:

Consider: the teenage girl with genital herpes whose future is ravaged by recurrent disease, who lives with the nagging fear of cancer, and who wonders whether her babies will be healthy; or the young woman whose pelvic abscess is "cured" by a total abdominal hysterectomy, who is robbed of future motherhood, and is dependent on hormone replacement for the rest of her life; or the young man who never heard of sexually transmitted hepatitis B until his liver biopsy showed the chronic active form of the disease. [36]

(Alcohol Use)

With the separation of religious principles, self-control has plummeted and alcohol abuse has become a significant national problem:

Alcohol Consumption Per Capita

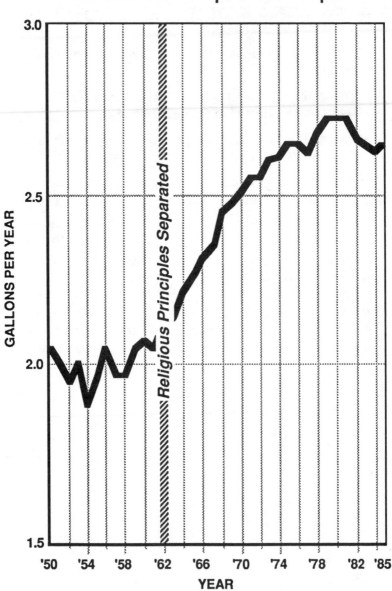

Basic data from National Clearinghouse for Alcohol Consumption.

How large a problem is alcohol abuse?

- According to the *Uniform Crime Report* from the Department of Justice, there were *over 4 million* alcohol-related arrests in 1988, an increase of 57 percent over the 2.6 million arrests of 1979. [37]

- According to a survey entitled *Drugs and the Nation's High School Students*, more than 9 out of 10 members of the high school class of 1985 had used alcohol. [38]

- Figures for "recent heavy drinking" for that same year revealed that 45 percent of boys and 25 percent of girls are heavy-drinkers. [39]

- A survey conducted by the Naval Health Research Center found that 42 percent of recent naval recruits said they "got drunk" at least once a week. [40]

- According to the 1984 "Gallup Youth Survey," teenagers say alcohol abuse is the second largest problem they face. [41]

- Every day in America, 437 children are arrested for drinking or drunken driving. [42]

(*Summary*)

Since the separation of religious principles from public affairs in 1962-63, violent crime offenses have risen over 500 percent; national productivity has dropped over 80 percent; the cases of sexually transmitted diseases are up nearly 200 percent; and per capita alcohol consumption has increased by over one-third. The three religion-related warnings given by Washington in his Farewell Address are worthy of review:

- apart from religion and morality there will be *no* respect for property or life;

- national morality *cannot* be maintained without religious principles; and

- a policy, to be a good policy, *must* include religion.

Washington, in that same Farewell Address, explained that religion and morality are the *foundation* of national political prosperity and then rhetorically questioned:

> Who that is a sincere friend to [government] can look with indifference upon attempts to shake the foundation of this [national] fabric? [43]

Can a true friend to America really be indifferent to what the Court has done in shaking America's foundation of religion and morality? Not in Washington's opinion!

Chapter 6
The Emergence of
New National Problems

In addition to the skyrocketing intensification of existing problems since 1962-63, brand new problems have erupted. The appearance of these new problems is documented in *Statistical Abstracts of the United States,* an annual compilation by the federal government of statistical data collected and tracked by the various departments (Departments of Commerce, Labor, Health and Human Services, Justice, Education, Agriculture, etc.).

When a brand new statistical category appears in the *Statistical Abstracts,* it indicates that there is a sufficient national awareness of that area to warrant its individual monitoring—i.e., it signals the birth of a new national problem. Prior to 1962, the recorded categories tended to remain constant from year to year—few new categories emerged. However, since 1962, many new categories have appeared.

For example, statistics first appeared on child abuse in 1976. This does not mean child abuse did not occur in previous years; it simply indicates that it was not widespread enough to be considered a serious national problem. Several of the newly intensified national problems include:

- Child abuse—up 240 percent since 1976;
- Corruption of public officials—up over 450 percent since 1973;
- Illegal drug abuse—up 1,375 percent since 1962;
- AIDs—a 43,300 percent increase since 1982;
- Sexual abuse of children—up nearly 2,300 percent since 1976;
- Illiteracy—currently the highest illiteracy rate of any industrial nation in the world.

These are only a few of the many new categories which have appeared in the *Statistical Abstracts* since the separation of religious principles from public affairs in 1962-63.

Child Abuse Reporting Rates

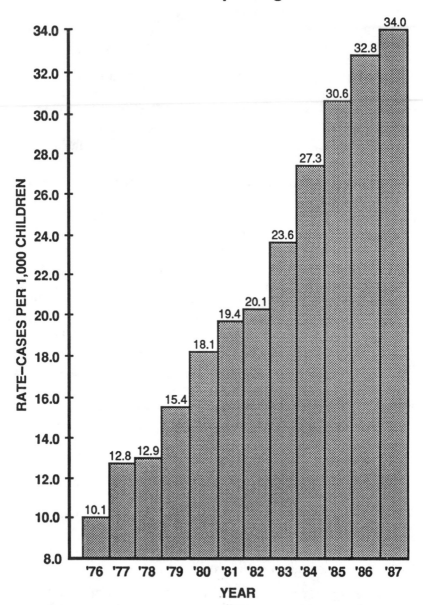

Basic data from *National Study on Child Neglect and Abuse Reporting*, annual. Provided by American Humane Association, Denver, CO.

Rate of Sexual Abuse of Children

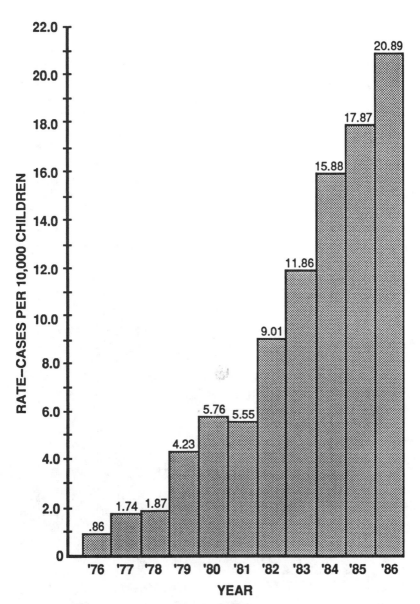

Basic data from *National Study on Child Neglect and Abuse Reporting,* annual. Provided by American Humane Association, Denver, CO.

Federal Prosecutions of Public Corruption

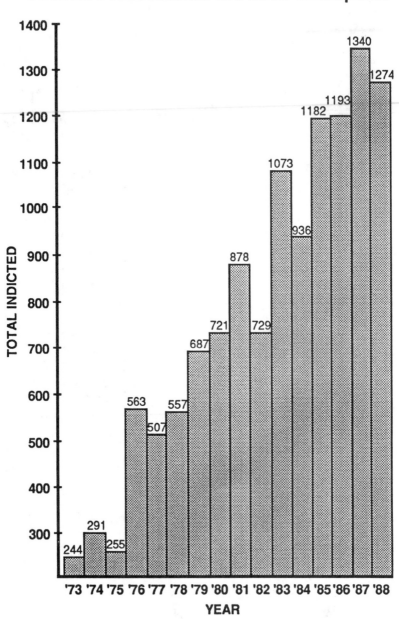

Basic data from *Statistical Abstracts of the United States.*

AIDS

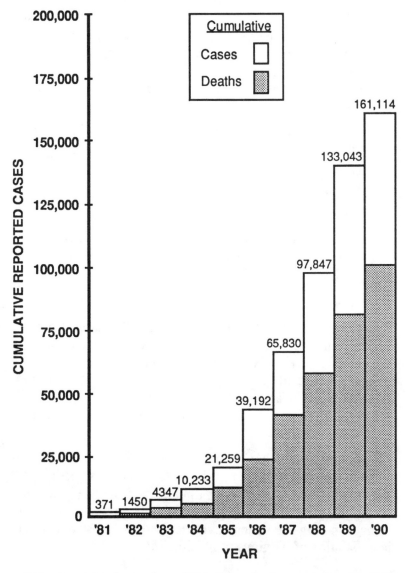

Collecting of data began June, 1981. Reporting began on June 15, 1982.

Basic data from *Aids Weekly Surveillance Report--United States,*
Center for Disease Control.

(*Drug Use*)

According to the National Institute on Drug Abuse, America has a level of involvement with illegal drugs higher than any other industrialized nation in the world. [1] Nearly two-thirds of American teenagers have used drugs before they finish high school, and 40 percent have used drugs other than marijuana. [2] According to a survey entitled *Drugs and the Nation's High School Students:* [3]

- More than half of the high school class of 1985 had tried marijuana;

- More than a quarter of the students reported using marijuana in the past month;

- One in six had used cocaine;

- One in eight had used hallucinogens, such as LSD;

- Most students using drugs made their initial decision to try a drug between 7th and 10th grades.

Additionally:

> A survey conducted by the Naval Health Research Center found that 48 percent of the recruits reported using marijuana in the six months before entering the service, and 42 percent said they "got drunk" at least once a week...Last year...the United States decertified 1,400 people from handling nuclear weapons because of drug and alcohol abuse. [4]

In the 1984 "Gallup Youth Survey," teenagers said drug abuse is the largest problem they face. [5] Adults agreed: in the 1987 Gallup poll, the American public said the use of drugs is the biggest problem facing public schools today. [6] Notice the changes in drug use which have occurred among students since the separation of religious principles: [7]

Youth Who Have Ever Used Illegal Drugs

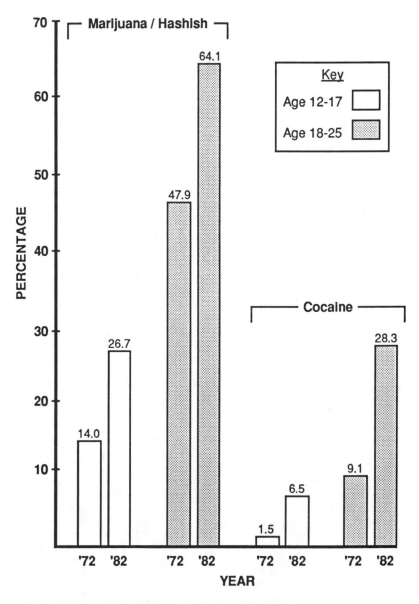

Basic data from *National Survey on Drug Abuse*,
provided by National Institute on Drug Abuse.

H.S. Seniors Who Had Tried Marijuana

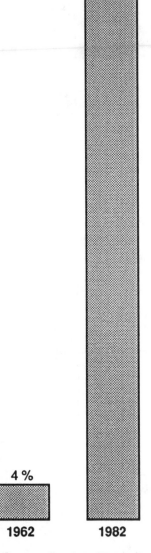

University Of Michigan Survey, *Reader's Digest,* August 1983, p.138.

(*Illiteracy*)

According to the National Institute of Education:

- Up to 72 million American adults are functional illiterates—unable to read or write above the 5th-grade level—and 26 million cannot read or write at all. [8]
- Illiteracy rates run as high as 47 percent for 17-year-old minority youths, 60 percent for prison inmates, and 75 percent for unemployed people. [9]
- The number of adult illiterates is increasing by about 2.3 million each year. [10]

According to Project Literacy U.S. (PLUS):

- The U.S. has the highest illiteracy rate among industrial nations.
- Nearly one million young Americans drop out of school every year.
- More than 70 million American adults never graduated from high school.
- Adult illiteracy costs the U.S. an estimated $225 billion yearly.

Functional illiterates commit many costly blunders. The Business Council for Effective Literacy in New York cites an insurance clerk who paid a claimant $2,200 on a $22 settlement because she didn't understand decimals; a steel-mill worker who misordered $1 million in parts because he could not read instructions well enough; a feed-lot laborer who misread a label and killed a pen of cattle by giving them poison instead of feed. [11]

According to statistics provided by the White House in September 1989, 700,000 high school students who *graduated from high-school* in 1986 alone *were not able to read their own diplomas!* While a high illiteracy rate might be expected in a third-world nation, it should not occur in the United States. Nevertheless, "the United States ranks 48th in adult literacy among the 149 countries represented at the United Nations,"[12] worst among industrial nations!

Chapter 7
National Accountability and Biblical Repercussions

The United States has long been touted as a world leader. However, after significant declines in so many areas, one could properly question how much of a leader the United States actually is. Nonetheless, despite the repudiation and separation of Godly principles from public affairs, America has continued to be a world leader—but in the wrong categories. Since 1962-63, the United States has become "number-one-in-the-world" in the following categories:

- Violent crime
- Divorce rate
- Teenage pregnancy rate (the western world's leader)
- Voluntary abortions
- Illegal drug use
- Illiteracy rate (the highest of any industrial nation)
- Documented cases of AIDs

Perhaps the best explanation for this reversal was given over 200 years ago during a time of frustration in the Constitutional Convention. The state delegates attending that Convention had fulfilled the proper requirements for office found in their own state constitutions. One of the provisions found in virtually every state constitution written by the Founders, both before and after the adoption of the federal Constitution, required the acknowledgment of a belief in future rewards and punishments:

And each member, before he takes his seat, shall make and subscribe the following declaration, viz.: "I do believe in one God, the creator and governor of the universe, the rewarder to the good and the punisher of the wicked." THE CONSTITUTIONS OF PENNSYLVANIA AND VERMONT

The qualifications of electors shall be [that he]... acknowledges the being of a God and believes in the future states of rewards and punishments. THE CONSTITUTION OF SOUTH CAROLINA

No person who denies the being of God, or a future state of rewards and punishments, shall hold any office in the civil department of this State. THE CONSTITUTION OF TENNESSEE

Excerpts of a similar nature from the other state's constitutions demonstrate that the Founders firmly believed in individual accountability to God—the understanding that each individual must one day stand before God Almighty and give an accounting for his actions, which would then result in rewards or punishments.

However, their discussions during the Constitutional Convention indicate that they not only understood personal accountability, they also understood national accountability to God. An individual's final reckoning with God will occur after departure from this life; it may occur immediately after death or 10,000 years after death; but it will occur—a final *future* reckoning is inevitable. However, a nation, unlike an individual, is not eternal—when a nation is gone, it is forever gone. Since a nation cannot account to God in the future, when does it account to God? The answer to that question was clearly articulated by delegate George Mason on the floor of the Constitutional Convention and is possibly the most significant explanation of what happened to this nation after 1962-63:

As nations cannot be rewarded or punished in the next world, so they must be in this. By an inevitable chain of causes and effects, Providence punishes national sins by national calamities. [1]

Nations account to God in the present—right now! The Bible is filled with accounts of how the stand taken by a nation's leaders can cause immediate crisis for the nation.

Consider the story of Elijah's conflict with the prophets of Baal on Mt. Carmel (1 Kings 18). Following his victory and the complete vindication of God, Elijah retreated to Mt. Horeb where he complained to God that he was the only righteous individual left in the nation. God promptly informed him that, no, he was not the only one left; there were still 7,000 men in the nation who had never bowed their knee to Baal—still 7,000 righteous men of integrity who had not compromised.

Yet, these 7,000 righteous men, just like every other individual in the nation, had just been through a three-and-one-half-year famine brought on the nation because of the wicked stands taken by Ahab and Jezebel, the nation's leaders. God dealt with the entire nation based on the actions of its leaders.

A second example of national accountability is seen when King David numbered the troops (1 Chronicles 21). David's numbering of the troops was an act of gloating in his own strength and military accomplishments—an act based on his assumption that the size of his army was responsible for his many victories. However, the reason for David's many victories had been God's direct assistance in the battles ("Horses are prepared against the day of battle, but *victory comes from the Lord!*" PROVERBS 21:31).

Somehow King David had forgotten who had brought him to his position of prominence. A similar situation was developing in America in 1787 until Benjamin Franklin rose on the floor of the Constitutional Convention and reminded the delegates:

> In the situation of this Assembly, groping, as it were, in the dark to find political truth, and scarce able to distinguish it when presented to us, how has it happened, Sir, that we have not hitherto once thought of humbly applying to the Father of lights to illuminate our understanding! In the beginning of the contest with Great Britain, when we were sensible of danger, we had daily prayer in this room for the Divine protection. —Our prayers, Sir, were heard, and they were graciously answered. All of us who were engaged in the struggle must have observed frequent instances of a superintending Providence in our favor...And have we now forgotten this powerful Friend? Or do we imagine we no

longer need His assistance? I have lived, Sir, a long time, and the longer I live, the more convincing proofs I see of this truth—that God governs in the affairs of men. And if a sparrow cannot fall to the ground without his notice, is it probable that an empire can rise without his aid? We have been assured, Sir, in the Sacred Writings, that "except the Lord build the house, they labor in vain that build it." I firmly believe this; and I also believe that without His concurring aid, we shall succeed in this political building no better than the builders of Babel...I therefore beg leave to move—that henceforth prayers imploring the assistance of Heaven, and its blessings on our deliberations, be held in this Assembly every morning before we proceed to business. [2]

Following this rebuke, the delegates entered a three day recess and completely refocused their attention and rededicated their minds to the Lord. For three days, they fasted, prayed, and invited ministers from across the city to address them and pray for them.

However, the delegates' response to Franklin's rebuke was quite different from the response of King David when General Joab discouraged him from numbering his troops (1 Chronicles 21:3). David ignored Joab's advice and ordered the count to be made. Consequently, as a result of David's stand which excluded any acknowledgment of God or of His hand, a plague befell the nation (1 Chronicles 21:14). The stand of the nation's leaders had again affected the entire nation.

Not only did George Mason and Benjamin Franklin express their understanding of this truth, but Thomas Jefferson, when discussing the wrongs of slavery and slave ownership, made a statement so important and so respected that it is engraved inside the Jefferson Memorial in Washington, D.C.:

Indeed, I tremble for my country when I reflect that God is just and that His justice cannot sleep forever. [3]

President Lincoln, as our nation's leader, understood the concept of national accountability to God. Once, on overhearing a clergyman say that he hoped "the Lord was on our side," Lincoln replied:

> I am not at all concerned about that, for I know that the Lord is always on the side of the right. But it is my constant anxiety and prayer that I and this nation should be on the Lord's side. [4]

It is vital that a nation's leaders take stands which cause God to remain an ally and not an enemy. Is it simply coincidence that each of the categories presented began to deteriorate visibly and dramatically immediately after the nation's leaders repudiated God and His principles? Or can it be that the principle of national accountability is at work?

The simple acknowledgment of God has provided us with more blessings and prosperity than we can suppose. The Bible clearly records God's promise: "Whoever honors me, I will honor. And whoever disregards me, I will disregard" (1 Samuel 2:30). When we were honoring God in our public affairs, we were elevated among the nations of the world in achievement, morality, productivity, stability, and reputation. Since disregarding Him, no longer are we a superior nation; our performances have lapsed into mediocrity when compared with other nations. The United States is still "Number One" in the world, but now in the wrong areas.

Psalms 91:14-16 chronicles what was happening to this nation when it was openly acknowledging God prior to 1962. In these verses, God declares:

> *I will protect him, for he acknowledges my name. He will call upon me, and I will answer him; I will be with him in trouble, I will deliver him and honor him, with long life will I satisfy him and show him my salvation.*

Notice the benefits of acknowledging God—benefits we were enjoying before 1962: *"I will answer him..."* Statistics on students, families, schools, and the nation demonstrated extraordinary stability. *"I will protect him..."* The remarkably low rates of crime, abuse, pregnancies, STDs, etc. evidence that we definitely were under Divine protection and blessing. *"I will be with him in trouble...*" We experienced declining divorce rates and fewer family breakups. *"With long life will I satisfy him..."* Suicide rates were low among students. *"I will honor him..."* We enjoyed a lofty international reputation, but have now become a nation embarrassed by its educational system, public corruption, illiteracy, immorality, child abuse, and drug use.

Jeremiah 8 elucidates the problems which occur when a nation rejects God as was done by the Court in 1962-63:

> *Since they have rejected the word of the Lord, what kind of wisdom do they have? Therefore I will give their wives to other men and their fields to new owners...They dress the wound of my people as though it were not serious, saying 'Peace, peace' when there is no peace...they have no shame at all; they do not even know how to blush. So they will fall among the fallen... I will take away their harvest, there will be no figs on the tree, and their leaves will wither. What I have given them will be taken away.*

Notice the accuracy of those verses: *"Since they have rejected the word of the Lord, what kind of wisdom do they have?"* Our academic achievements have plummeted in both domestic and international testing. *"Therefore I will give their wives to other men..."* Adultery has risen three to four times its previous level. *"...and their fields to new owners..."* Defaults on payments and repossession of property have skyrocketed; there were 595,000 bankruptcies in 1988 alone. [5] *"They dress the wound of my people as though it were not serious, saying 'Peace, peace' when there is no peace..."* Our nation downplays the enormity of its problems and attempts to treat superficially the symptoms of serious problems such as illiteracy, poor academic achievement, STDs, etc., while ignoring their root causes. *"They have no shame at all; they do not even know how to blush..."* Morality is a word with new parameters: things previously done only in secret, and never discussed, are now done openly, with little or no embarrassment. Now, when speaking of "gay" clothing or a "gay" party, one no longer means "jolly and happy" but describes an entire subculture based on immorality. *"So they will fall among the fallen..."* Our international positions in education, industry, morality, and family stability have fallen to the worst levels of any industrial nation. *"I will take away their harvest, there will be no figs on the tree, and their leaves will wither..."* Our productivity has dropped almost 80 percent from its pre-1962 levels. *"What I have given them will be taken away..."* Major reversals have occurred in most areas since God and His principles were barred from public affairs.

When contemplating His treatment by the nation's leaders, God asked a probing question in Jeremiah 7:

> *Am I the one they are provoking? Are they not rather harming themselves to their own shame?*

The prohibition on Christian principles in public affairs did nothing to harm God; it obviously has scandalized the entire nation. The words of Franklin's rebuke to the Constitutional Convention again come to mind:

> Have we now forgotten this powerful Friend? Or do we imagine we no longer need His assistance?...without His concurring aid, we shall succeed...no better than the builders of Babel; we shall be divided by our little, partial local interests; our projects will be confounded; and we ourselves shall become a reproach and a byword down to future ages. [6]

The practice of public prayer and of seeking God's "concurring aid" was integral to this nation's birth, growth, development and maturing. We were born and guided through our adolescence, and then brought through turmoil and on to stability by men of prayer and religious principle. Can we possibly believe that what was gained by prayer and religious principle can be maintained without them? To deny students the access to those Christian principles which made our nation great is to deny them the opportunity to participate in our national heritage. Recall Washington's question:

> Who that is a sincere friend to [America] can look with indifference upon attempts to shake the foundation of this [nation's] fabric? [7]

As proven by the graphs and statistics in this book, prayer in schools and the acknowledgment of God in public affairs is not simply a religious issue—it is a national issue! Obtaining God's aid and favor by simply acknowledging Him in public is an asset not to be underestimated; we can ill afford to attempt to continue without His aid and favor. Hosea 6:3 again needs to become the description of our national policy:

"Let us press on to acknowledge Him."

Chapter 8
An Analysis of the Problem

In order to determine an effective strategy for recovering from the effects of the Court's rulings, we need to isolate the specific consequences of those rulings. The first and most obvious effect of the Court's ban on the acknowledgment of God and the use of His principles in public affairs was that the Court had directly challenged God. Moreover, the Court was strongly unified in its repudiation of Him—only one Justice dissented. Never before had an official government voice opposed and censured God in public affairs. This posture taken by the Court triggered the law of national accountability and subjected the nation to its consequences.

The second effect of the Court's repudiation of the use of Godly principles in public affairs was the loss of the personal benefits derived from living by Godly principles. As explained in Deuteronomy 6:24 and 10:13:

> The Lord commanded us to obey all these decrees *so that we might always prosper.*

> Observe the Lord's decrees *for your own good.*

His principles are for *our* benefit—to keep *us* alive, to cause *us* to prosper, to cause *us* to enjoy life. When His commands are rejected, it is to our own harm.

To understand that these two effects directly relate to our current national disgrace is to begin to understand what must be done to recover. The adage that "recognizing the problem is half the battle" is certainly applicable in this situation. However, it would be negligent to take restorative actions without first identifying the original cause of the problem—i.e., to identify what caused the Court to behave as it did in 1962. Not to recognize these root causes will invite future repetition.

The graphs clearly illustrate that the 1962 ban on religious principles and the acknowledgment of God in public affairs precipitated the declines with which we now struggle. Yet, when 97 percent of the nation claimed a belief in God in 1962, how could the nation allow the elimination of God from schools? Can the downturns so evident on the graphs properly be blamed on the Justices who made the rulings? Unfortunately, the Court cannot be used as the scapegoat.

While the Doctrine of Separation which now dominates the Court's rulings is of recent origin and had never been "raised" as an issue in education until the 1962 decision,[1] the rulings would never have occurred had not the Christian community-at-large voluntarily removed itself from the political, social, and legal arenas prior to 1962. When non-Christians and the ungodly dominate public offices, it should come as no surprise that their rulings and public policies would also be non-Christian and ungodly.

The following excerpts from the constitutions of the states which participated in the original Constitutional Convention reveal what the Founders believed about public office and public policy:

> [Everyone appointed to public office must say]: "I...do profess faith in God the Father, and in Jesus Christ His only Son, and in the Holy Ghost, one God, blessed for evermore; and I do acknowledge the Holy Scriptures of the Old and New Testament to be given by Divine inspiration."—DELAWARE CONSTITUTION, 1776 [2]

> No person, who should deny the being of God, or the truth of the [Christian] religion, or the divine authority either of the Old or New Testaments, or who shall hold religious principles incompatible with the freedom and safety of the state, shall be capable of holding any office, or place of trust or profity in the civil department within this state.—NORTH CAROLINA CONSTITUTION, 1776 [3]

> Morality and piety, rightly grounded on evangelical principles...give the best and greatest security to government...therefore...the people of this state...empower the legislature...to authorize...the support and maintenance of public [Christian] teachers of piety, religion, and morality.—NEW HAMPSHIRE CONSTITUTION, 1784, 1792 [4]

These excerpts were not isolated portions of obscure laws, nor were they "mistakes." Eleven of the thirteen colonies had similar laws on record at the time of the Constitutional Convention. Many of these laws remained in force for over a hundred years *after* the ratification of the Constitution. Can there be any doubt that the framers of these state constitutions, who also became the framers of the U.S. Constitution, believed Christians were the ones to govern, the ones to maintain the freedoms provided by God in our form of government?

The Founders never intended to separate Christianity from government, only to keep a single denomination from running the nation. They wanted to preclude the possibility that what happened in Great Britain might happen in America (the establishment of a single Christian *denomination* such as Anglicanism or Catholicism as the *only* national denomination). Consequently, the First Amendment was passed, which simply states:

> Congress shall make no law regarding the establishment of religion or prohibiting the free exercise thereof.

The words "separation," "church," or "state" do not even appear in the First Amendment! The First Amendment simply sought to prohibit the federal government from declaring the entire nation to be *only* Catholic, *only* Baptist, *only* Methodist, etc. The Founders *never* intended that Christian principles be divorced from public affairs. By the plan and intent of the Founders, Christians, and therefore Christian principles, had remained intimately involved in the political, judicial, and educational realms.

However, in the 1920's-1930's, Christians began to isolate themselves from public affairs. The encouragement of many Christian leaders became: "Let others be politicians; we will concern ourselves only with saving souls."

Churches began to encourage their young people to enter seminaries and become pastors or missionaries and discouraged them from entering the legal arena, politics, or public life. Then slowly—little by little—the church-at-large began not only to believe but also to teach the heresy that Christianity and politics should be divorced. Consequently, Christians voluntarily relinquished political and judicial positions and responsibilities to the ungodly who did not hold precious the beliefs that had shaped and guided the nation for almost two centuries.

The new ungodly replacements began to introduce new ideas and laws contrary to our heritage and values; the church took little action to stop them—it was being involved in the "spiritual." The seclusion of the "spiritual" from everyday life and activities not only insulted our heritage, it was a Biblical error:

He who isolates himself seeks his own selfish desires; he rages against all sound judgment. PROVERBS 18:1

Christians, through bad doctrine, political inactivity, and apathy, handed the reins of the nation into the hands of men not holding the belief that God was important to or should be involved in the public affairs of the nation. These new politicians awarded lifelong appointments to Justices not only willing, but eager to uproot the Christian practices that had been the heart of this nation for centuries. The Court's 1962 (and subsequent) decisions were merely an outgrowth of what the Christian community-at-large had permitted and encouraged preceding those rulings.

A parable told by Jesus in Matthew 13:24-26 describes this process. In that parable, there were good people who had a good field which was growing good seed. However, an enemy came in and planted bad seeds among the good, thus contaminating the entire field. What afforded the enemy an opportunity to damage the good? The stark answer is found in verse 24: "But while everyone was sleeping, the enemy came." Very bluntly, *first* the church—the Christians—went to sleep, and *then* the enemy came and caused the damage.

Having, by our own abdication, transferred a nation which was so firmly built on Godly principles into the hands of unGodly men, should we really be surprised by what has happened? The problems we have created for ourselves are evident, yet there is a solution.

Chapter 9
What Can Be Done Now?

Having seen the havoc loosed since 1962, what can be done to slow it, or better yet, reverse it? The obvious solution would be to undo what was done. Yet, how can the past three decades be undone? There is no way to reduce the trauma to the already damaged and destroyed lives, no way to restore the broken families, nor to remove the guilt of their personal failures. While it is impossible to turn back the clock and recoup the losses, it is possible to begin significant recovery and to move in a positive direction.

Solutions for what has occurred in America since 1962-63 must center on reversing the two-pronged impact from the Court's ruling: (1) the official stand taken against God must be repealed, and (2) the utilization of religious principles in public affairs must be restored. There are at least eleven specific activities which can help realize these goals. However, any strategy for recovery must ultimately be guided by Scriptural principles if it is to be successful. As pointed out in Joshua 1:8:

> Be careful to do everything written in [this Book of the Law]. *Then* you will be prosperous and successful.

[1] According to the Bible, what must be the initial step in any strategy to recover what we have lost?

> I exhort therefore, that, *first of all*, supplications, prayers, intercessions, and giving of thanks, be made for all men; for *[leaders] and for all that are in authority.* 1 TIMOTHY 2:1

This is not an arbitrary, haphazard plan given by God. God wants prayer for the civic leaders *first*, because civic leaders affect the life of every remaining individual in the entire nation. For our own benefit, we should be praying regularly for our leaders at the local, state, and federal levels in each branch of government: (1) judges and appointed officials, (2) elected representatives, and (3) the executives—President, Governor, Mayor and other chief officials.

Furthermore, we need to pray _now_ for God to raise up Godly candidates and to place them into office in the next election. Since "an ounce of prevention is worth a pound of cure," having the right type of individuals in office can prevent the enactment of many damaging policies.   As explained by William Penn:

> Governments, like clocks, go from the motion men give them...Wherefore governments rather depend upon men, than men upon governments...Let men be good, and the government cannot be bad. [1]

Pray for our leaders on every level, and pray for God to root out the wicked from office and to raise up righteous individuals to replace them.   **Item #1—Become active in praying for leaders and officials at all levels!** □

2 Voluntary prayer may not be allowed in schools now, but that does not mean children should not be trained to pray daily. If you have children of school age, pray with them daily before they leave for school.   Show them the importance of prayer and petition, and help them begin each day by seeking God. **Item #2—Become active in praying with your children!** □

3 Song of Solomon 8:13 declares: "Your companions hearken to your voice, so speak!" You _can_ be effective with your friends and with others.   Enlarge your sphere of influence and organize small groups for prayer for students, families, schools and the nation.   God wants such prayers:

> The prayer of the upright is His delight. PROVERBS 15:8
> Pray without ceasing. 1 THESSALONIANS 5:17
> Continue in prayer. COLOSSIANS 4:2

Prayer will be the first key to effecting significant and lasting change. Situations will not change on earth until they have been changed in the heavenlies. As Jesus taught: _"Thy_ Kingdom come, _Thy_ will be done, _on earth as it is_ in Heaven."   **Item #3—Become active in praying with others!** □

| 4 | Children do not currently obtain historically accurate information from schools, educational institutions, or the public media about the role of Christians in the nation and the importance of involving God in our public affairs; however, *you* can help them obtain this information. If you have children, teach them the Christian history, heritage, and traditions of our nation. Help them to recognize that the current Doctrine of Separation is hostile toward Christianity and that it is unfounded and that it is wrong. If you do not have children, then begin to educate those around you to the true history of our nation. (A list of recommended reading/resource books containing accurate history is included in Appendix B). **Item #4—Become active in teaching the truth!** □

| 5 | The political realm, formerly dominated by Christians, is still available to them. The use of politics resulted in the elimination of God from public affairs; it can restore Him. We must remove officials who do not comply with traditional, historical and Biblical principles and replace them with those who do. While it might seem easier to empty the ocean with a thimble than to change politics, it is actually not as difficult as it appears.

Just as Christians incorrectly believed we must isolate ourselves from politics, we have also incorrectly believed that we don't have the power to change things. "I'm only an individual—one vote. What can I do?" "My vote won't make a difference anyway." "It does us no good to vote. As Christians, we're already in the minority." Sound familiar? We've probably heard these statements, or perhaps said them ourselves. The fact is, they are *not* true.

A Gallup poll released in July 1988 shows that 84 percent of this nation firmly believes in Jesus Christ. A separate poll indicates that 94 percent believe in God. Only 16 percent do not believe strongly in Jesus and a meager 6 percent deny the existence of God. Yet we have been led to believe that we, the 84 percent, are the minority. We are not! It is time to declare that the 6 percent will not abrogate the rights of the 94 percent!

The Constitution makes it clear that numbers are important. This is to be a government of a majority of the people, by the majority of the people, and for a majority of the people. Every vote taken in the House or the Senate will eventually result in a majority and a minority. Because there will be a minority and a majority on every issue, someone's wishes or "rights" always will be "violated" on any vote which is not unanimous; nevertheless, the rights of the majority are *never* to be set aside by a lesser number.

Imagine a hypothetical vote in the U.S. Senate where the final tally was 94 to 6. It would not only be absurd, it would be untenable for the 6 to be declared the winner and to have their policy enacted over the votes of the 94; yet this is exactly what happened when the acknowledgment of God was prohibited. Can such an act truly be appropriate in a republic (to which we pledge our allegiance), a democracy (which we most often claim to be), or in a democratic-republic (which is a combination of the two)? Obviously not!

Nevertheless, this same scenario is repeated often in this nation today. Consider these numbers which not only have appeared in various polls in recent years, but also have remained relatively constant over the past two decades:

- 82 percent of the nation wants prayer back in school;
- 82 percent of the nation opposes homosexual rights;
- 70 percent of the nation wants creation taught in science classes;
- 68 percent of the nation opposes the use of abortion as a means of convenience birth control.

Other categories could be named; the results are the same. We have relinquished our right to be a democratic-republic and instead have become an oligarchy (the rule of a nation by a small group or council of elite individuals). Why? Because the majority has yet to realize that it is the majority. The majority acts like a minority and doesn't get involved.

The key that will enable Christians to change politics is to change our attitude. Proverbs 23:7 declares: "As he thinks in his heart, so is he." As long as Christians continue to believe that we are a minority, we will continue to act like one. When Christians begin to believe that we are a majority—the 84 percent—then we will begin to act like a majority, and then we *will* make a difference.

Proof of this came in five separate U.S. Senate races in 1986. The five candidates who stood for returning Godly principles to public affairs were defeated by a collective total of only 57,000 collective votes—less than 12,000 votes per state. Yet in those same five states in 1986, there were *over 5 million Christians* who did not even vote! If only 1 of every 100 *non-voting Christians* —only one percent—had voted for the candidate supporting Godly principles, these five men would have been elected and would have created a ten-vote swing in the Senate toward restoring Godly principles to public affairs: five ungodly men would have been retired and five Godly men would have taken their place.

While this might seem like a disheartening report, really it is very encouraging. It shows that activists and radicals didn't defeat the Godly candidates; those Godly candidates were defeated by *inactive Christians!* We *do* have power! We *can* make a difference! We must recognize our potential and act like a majority. When the 82 percent who want prayer returned to school begin to act like 82 percent, things will change! The ability to change the situation is in *our* hands! As Edward Burke explained:

> All that is necessary for evil to triumph is for good men
> to do nothing.[2]

The overwhelming majority of our citizens are ready to return God to public affairs; yet, the overwhelming majority of our elected officials are not. Whose fault is that? Is it the fault of our elected legislators? Clearly not, since we are the ones who elected them! We—the Christian community—must bear most of the responsibility for what has happened. Notice President James Garfield's explanation of this truth:

Now, more than ever before, the people are responsible for the character of their Congress. If that body be ignorant, reckless, and corrupt, it is because the people tolerate ignorance, recklessness, and corruption. If it be intelligent, brave, and pure, it is because the people demand these high qualities to represent them in the national legislature.[3]

John Jay, America's first Chief Justice of the Supreme Court and one of the three men most responsible for the adoption of the Constitution, advised in a letter on October 12, 1816:

Providence has given to our people the choice of their rulers. It is the duty, as well as the privilege and interest, of a Christian nation to select and prefer Christians for their rulers.[4]

On another occasion, Jay received a letter from a friend who asked him whether it was proper to vote for an ungodly candidate. Jay responded on January 1, 1813:

Whether our religion permits Christians to vote for infidel rulers is a question which merits more consideration than it seems yet to have generally received, either from the clergy or the laity. It appears to me that what the prophet said to Jehoshaphat about his attachment to Ahab ("Shouldest thou help the ungodly and love them that hate the Lord?" 2 Chron. 19:2) affords a salutary lesson.[5]

Noah Webster delivered a similar admonition:

Let it be impressed on your mind that God commands you to choose for rulers just men who will rule in the fear of God...if the citizens neglect their duty and place unprincipled men in office, the government will soon be corrupted...If a republican government fails to secure public prosperity and happiness, it must be because the citizens neglect the Divine commands, and elect bad men to make and administer the laws.[6]

Charles Finney, a prominent Christian leader in the early 1800's, succinctly declared:

> The time has come that Christians must vote for honest men, and take consistent ground in politics or the Lord will curse them...God cannot sustain this free and blessed country, which we love and pray for, unless the Church will take right ground. [7]

The dilemma now facing us as Christians is similar to the dilemma faced by a group in the Bible who, like us today, were experiencing severe national problems that were affecting their personal lives. As those individuals contemplated their course of action, they concluded, as should we, that involvement was the only reasonable alternative. Or, as they so aptly quipped in 2 Kings 7:3:

> Why sit we here 'til we die?

It's time to believe and behave differently. We are *not* a minority; we are the majority! We *can* make a difference! Our vote *does* count! **Item #5—Become an active voter!** □

[6] Too often, a seemingly "good" candidate is elected and we later end up regretting his public stands and votes. Much of this could be eliminated if the right questions were asked *before* election. We need to know more about a candidate than his professional qualifications—we need to know the *personal* beliefs which qualify him to represent us. As pointed out in a famous book about George Washington, released in 1800:

> A public character is often an artificial one. It is not, then, in the glare of public, but in the shade of private life, that we are to look for the man. Private life is always real life. Behind the curtain, where the eyes of the million are not upon him, and where a man can have no motive but inclination, no incitement but honest nature, there he will always be sure to act himself: consequently, if he act greatly, he must be great indeed. Hence it has been justly said, that, "our private deeds, if

noble, are noblest of our lives."...it is the private virtues that lay the foundation of all human excellence. [8]

While there are many ways to ascertain a candidate's stand, two are readily available to any individual or group. The first is outside monitoring and the second is direct questioning.

Outside monitoring. Many national groups track major issues of concern to the Christian community and publish a voter's guide showing the federal voting record of the incumbents on these issues. Most of these national groups also have area coordinators who investigate the state/local races. (Information on how to contact several of these groups may be obtained in Appendix A). Contact the group's national headquarters to get the voting guides, and then ask for the name of their representative in your area. This representative will make available information on candidates in your state. While some local regions may not have a representative from each of the national monitoring groups, there is usually at least one of the groups which *will* have a contact in your area. It may take calls to several of the groups before you finally make the local connection you need, but don't give up!

Direct Questioning. Another way to obtain information on a candidate is simply to phone his(her) office; he will inform you where he stands on the issues. In addition to any questions you might ask on specific state or local issues, there are three more questions which will usually identify the guiding philosophy of that candidate. Question candidates on:

- Their views on God and government,
- Their views on abortion,
- Their views on homosexual behavior.

Their answers to these three questions will reveal whether they understand the importance of God's principles in government, whether they understand the value of a life, and whether they understand fundamental rights and wrongs. If they understand these three areas, then they probably have the proper foundation from which other political decisions may be properly made.

Determining the stands of area candidates is a project that can easily be undertaken by any individual or group—e.g., a men's or women's prayer fellowship, a home Bible study, a Sunday School class, etc.   First, contact the political parties' headquarters in your area and request a list of their candidates who will appear on the ballot, along with their mailing addresses and phone numbers.   Second, determine the questions you want to ask each candidate and then create a survey sheet containing those questions.   Third, mail that sheet to each candidate along with an enclosed letter requesting that he respond and return the survey by a specific date, at which time you will compile the results and distribute them throughout the community and in each church.   Fourth, once you have determined the candidates' stands, do all you can to publicize their positions.

(For a church to compile such a questionnaire and distribute the results does *not* violate any tax-exempt requirement of the IRS.   Simply educate the public to the candidates' stands on issues of concern to Christians; do not endorse a candidate or a party.   An educational publication *will not* jeopardize a church's tax-exempt status!)

No matter what position a candidate is seeking, scrutinize his/her stands.   Some candidates will argue that since they are seeking only the position of justice-of-the-peace, city-treasurer, dogcatcher, etc., that their stands on issues like abortion will have no bearing on their office.   While that statement may seem innocuous, it is misleading.   Since low-level local offices frequently have been stepping stones for many prominent national careers, the innate character and beliefs of any elected official is important at every level.

Therefore, examine *every* candidate's stands on moral and religious values; screen candidates thoroughly at the lowest levels of government where their election or defeat is easiest. Once a candidate is in office and becomes an incumbent, statistics show that his reelection is very likely.

Understand that a candidate may not agree with you on every doctrinal item; that is not important.   The determining factor is,

"Do we agree on the moral essentials?" Alexis de Tocqueville, in his famous 1836 book *Democracy in America* (still available in bookstores today), described the common thread important among differing denominations:

> The [denominations] which exist in the United States are innumerable. They all differ in respect to the worship which is due from man to his Creator; but they all agree in respect to the duties which are due from man to man. Each sect adores the Deity in its own peculiar manner; but all the sects preach the same moral law in the name of God...Almost all the sects of the United States are comprised within the great unity of Christianity, and Christian morality is everywhere the same. [9]

This nation will *not* be put back on track by Baptists alone, or by Catholics alone, or by Methodists alone, or by Pentecostals alone, or by any other single group; there is not enough strength in any one denomination to return America to its Biblical roots. However, it *will* be put back on track by *Christians*. **Item #6— Become active in investigating candidates!** ☐

7 Once you have determined which candidate is best for the position, there is more you can do. Generally, the candidate who is the best Christian selection will not receive good media coverage. However, this is *not* an insurmountable problem. A candidate can overcome media influence when he has strong grass-roots efforts—i.e., average people carrying his message and qualifications to other average people. It is not uncommon for a candidate with strong grass-roots help to win, despite the media coverage (or lack thereof) which he receives.

When you find a candidate who can make a difference in your community, state, or nation, get involved with him. Offer whatever financial support you can, and call his office and volunteer some of your time to help; he will be very appreciative and very responsive. By volunteering to help a Godly candidate, even if it is only for an hour or two, you will, in fact, be helping yourself and your posterity by helping to restore the nation.

The party of the candidate should make little difference. You might have been "born a Democrat"; you might have been "born a Republican"; you might have been "born an Independent"; it doesn't matter. The fact is, you were reborn a Christian; reflect that in your political involvement! Get involved with solid Christian candidates no matter what their party. **Item #7—Become active in helping candidates!** □

8 Another way to produce a change is to contact your Congressman directly. For too long, most Americans have underestimated the effect they can have, and thus have remained silent on the issues. It does *not* take many letters to make a difference. A sincere, personal letter expressing to him your views and your concerns *is* effective.

In June 1989, I had opportunity to participate in the introduction of a significant federal legislative bill. After its introduction, it was referred to the appropriate Congressional committee for hearings and discussion. However, two of the members of the committee refused to allow any hearings or any discussion on the bill; they were determined to let it die in committee.

The bill had already received support from a wide variety of Congressmen; in fact, in the preceding month, the House of Representatives had voted two-to-one in *favor* of the material in the proposed bill. Because of such widespread support, and because it seemed inappropriate for only two individuals to block the progress of the bill, we asked several of the Congressmen what could be done to get those two men to release the bill from the committee. The Congressmen instructed us to find individuals in those two men's home districts and get them to write letters to the two Congressmen, requesting them to release the bill and schedule hearings on it.

To determine how much mail was needed, we queried several: "Congressman, how do you know when you have a 'hot' issue?" Their answer was startling: "If we get as many as fifty letters on a bill, it's a very hot issue." They further indicated that, in their opinion, twenty letters would be sufficient to cause the two Congressmen to reverse their position on the bill.

Amazed, we continued: "How many letters do you usually receive on a bill?" They responded, "Five to ten is normal." The fact that five to ten letters is the norm on an issue is a compelling commentary on the inactivity of most individuals! Each Congressman represents at least 500,000 individuals, and only 20 letters can cause him to reverse his stand! It is for this reason that philosophical minorities and anti-Christian groups are often so successful in reaching their goals in Congress— they are simply more active than the majority in generating individual contacts with a Congressman.

Another illustration of how few individuals actually communicate with their legislator comes from a U.S. Congressman in a northwestern state. In 1990, in the closing weeks of the 101st Congress, one of the especially "hot" items to be dealt with was the federal budget. There had been stalemate after stalemate in negotiations between Congress and the White House; several volatile proposals were offered for cutting the budget, which produced open wrath and hostility from the public. Suggestions had been offered on raising taxes, on cutting Social Security, Medicare, salaries of federal workers, etc.—items particularly sensitive to large portions of the nation.

The Congressman's staff knew that the budget was a "hot" item because of the number of constituent phone calls which had "poured" into his office over a five-week period. How many calls had "poured in" over the five weeks? Six! His office had received a total of *six calls* about the budget over the five weeks, thus convincing him that this was a "hot" issue to his constituents! When a legislator is accustomed to receiving little or no communication from constituents on most issues, six calls can *seem* like a flood.

Conversations with Congressmen revealed the same policy: mass-produced mailings, form letters, or petitions get no response and usually go into the trash. If a person does not feel strongly enough about a bill to cause him to express himself in a personal, original letter, then he is not given much serious consideration. But when a Congressman gets a personal letter from an interested individual, it receives his attention; he simply does not receive many of these letters. It is important that you *personally* express your desires and concerns to your Congressman—a *personal* letter is effective, even a short one.

Letter writing is easy and often takes much less time than imagined. Usually, the difficulty is simply in getting started; once you begin the letter, your thoughts and feelings flow easily. Here are a few suggestions to assist you in effective letter writing:

- Be personal in your letter. Use the name of your Congressman—*don't* address it to "Dear Congressman". You typically don't appreciate mail addressed to "Dear Occupant"; neither does he. Call him/her by name; for example, Congressman Harry Jones, Congresswoman Jane Jackson, etc. (You can obtain the name of your Congressman through the library, Chamber of Commerce, or other similar public service organizations).

- Get to the point. Three or four paragraphs is plenty—don't be long-winded or wordy. Begin with a short, friendly greeting, then explain why you are writing and what you would like the Congressman to do. Close with a statement of appreciation (for his service, for his consideration of your request, etc.) and ask for a response to your letter.

- Be specific in your requests. Try to give the name, number, or description of the bill or measure with which you are concerned. Do *not* ask him to do general things like bring world peace, end the famines in Africa, etc.; he can no more do that than you can.

- Don't get preachy. Give practical, well-thought-out, logical reasons for your position and why you want him to take certain steps. Don't use Christian clichés or phrases.

- Don't threaten. Don't tell him, for example, that if he doesn't vote the way you want that you will never vote for him again, or that if he doesn't stop abortion that he will stand before God and answer for his votes. Although these things may be true, Philippians 2:14 instructs us to do everything without threatening. Threats tend to bring out the stubborn side in most individuals.

• Be complimentary and appreciative, not antagonistic, provoking, rude or abrasive. The Bible says not to speak evil of a ruler (Acts 23:5) and that a soft word breaks down the hardest resistance (Proverbs 25:15). Sincerely and genuinely thank him.

The address for your federal Representative or Senator is:

Name of your Representative
U.S. House of Representatives
Washington, DC, 20515

Name of your Senator
U.S. Senate
Washington, DC, 20510

It is very effective—and relatively easy—to organize a church or home letter-writing group. Many churches now set aside a portion of one service per month for their members to write letters to their Congressmen.

The church leadership may designate one (or several) individuals to research current bills of concern to the Christian community. The church then provides information on one bill to the congregation during a service and provides the members with the paper and the time necessary to jot a short personal note to their Congressmen on that bill/issue. This entire process usually requires only 10-15 minutes.

Since it often requires no more than twenty letters to have substantial impact, virtually any Sunday School or home-meeting group should easily be able to generate more than enough letters on a single bill to create a "crisis" for a Congressman!

Letters are more effective than calls, but calls are still effective. If you decide to call instead of write, call the Capitol switchboard at (202)-224-3121. When the operator answers, ask for your Senator or Representative by name. When a member of his office staff answers, ask to speak to your Congressman. If he is available, often he will speak with you. If he is unavailable, simply express to his staff your concern, or how you want him to vote on a particular issue. The staff *will* record your feelings and *will* communicate them to the Congressman. **Item #8—Become active in communicating with your elected officials!** □

⏐9⏐ Recent studies have shown that 92 percent of those working in the public media do not consider themselves "conservative" and nearly nine-out-of-ten support moral stands which most Christians oppose.[10] Furthermore, 66 percent feel that they have a personal responsibility to educate the public with *their* views.[11] In other words, the majority of those in media consider themselves to be "evangelists" of liberal views. Consequently, with a steady presentation of the liberal agenda, Christians do not hear about our victories (and we *do* have many). This is why Christians feel that they are a minority (although actual statistics disprove it) and that they have no power to influence the stands of government.

An effective way for Christians to present news and views on the other side is through the "Letters to the Editor" section of your local newspaper. Most papers allow opposing viewpoints in the "Letters to the Editor" section; take advantage of it. Your views can offer an alternative to those frequently presented by the media. Commit yourself to writing one or two letters a month.

When composing a public letter, be sure to avoid being purely emotional and avoid using Christian clichés and phrases—they communicate only to other well-informed Christians and not to the general population. In an English newspaper, you would not write in Japanese, nor would you write in Chinese; therefore, don't write in Christian-ese. Christian-ese is just as foreign a language to many readers as is Chinese or Japanese. Adopt the philosophy of Paul explained in 1 Corinthians 9:19-22:

"To everyone to win as many as possible...I became like one under the law so as to win those under the law. To those not having the law I became like one not having the law so as to win those not having the law. To the weak I became weak, to win the weak. I have become all things to all men so that by all possible means I might save some."

Utilize the opportunity to give sound, practical reasons for your opinions and to provide a basis for why others should adopt your views. As 1 Peter 3:15 instructs: "Be ready to give an answer to everyone." **Item #9—Get informed, then become active in educating others!** ☐

10 As you become more and more active and involved, don't underestimate the effect of the experience you are gaining. Be willing to become a leader by informing the community of issues and information, by recruiting others to run for office, by working for a sound candidate, or by running for local offices yourself.

Don't be afraid to run for a position on the local school board, city council, or other areas where you can begin to implement changes. Local offices are important—they influence the entire community, and it is easier to be elected to local government or to local school boards than to be elected to a statewide or national office. While Charles Finney's statement from the mid-1800s is appropriate for every level, it is especially true at the local level:

The church must take right ground in regard to politics... Politics are part of a religion in such a country as this and Christians must do their duty to the country as a part of their duty to God...[God] will bless or curse this nation according to the course [Christians] take [in politics]. [12]

Government won't be redeemed from without, it must be redeemed *from within* by people of Christian principle and integrity. God wants His people in all areas of government. **Item #10—Become active in leading community change!** ☐

[11] For the most part, our culture today has developed a short-term mentality. Our entertainment convinces us that a family or a national crisis can arise and be completely resolved in a 30- or 60-minute program. We have developed impatience as a national characteristic.

We often apply that same impatience to involvement in public affairs. We get involved in an election, maybe two, but when it doesn't completely turn around, we have a tendency to throw up our hands, declare that we tried and that it didn't make any difference, then move on to the next endeavor.

It took nearly half-a-century to arrive at the situation we are in today; even if the recovery is just as lengthy, it *will* come if we faithfully persist. The promise of Galatians 6:9 is that we will reap the benefits *if* we will simply "hang in there." The principle of slowly and steadily retaking lost ground, while neither appealing nor gratifying to our natural impatience, is a well-articulated Biblical principle:

> I *will not* drive them out in a single year...*Little by little*
> I *will* drive them out before you, until you have increased
> enough to take possession of the land. EXODUS 23:29-30

> The Lord your God *will* drive out [them] before you...
> *little by little.* You *will not* be allowed to eliminate them
> all at once. DEUTERONOMY 7:22

To retake the lost ground quickly is not the strategy prescribed by the Lord Himself; the rewards promised in the Scriptures go to the *faithful* (Matthew 25:21, 23). Commit yourself to this engagement for the long haul—for the duration. Equip yourself with the mentality of a marathon runner, not a sprinter. Very simply, be willing to compete until you win. **Item #11— Develop a long-term resolute spirit!** □

We have allowed the very principles which produce morality and virtue, and thus stability, to be banned from public life. We must regain the conviction that Christian principles are vital to national success, and we must be willing to pursue their reinstatement. We should adopt the philosophy stated so well by Benjamin Franklin:

> *He who shall introduce into public affairs*
> *the principles of primitive Christianity*
> *will change the face of the world.* [13]

Appendix A
Resource Groups

The following is a list of some of the organizations which track and report on diverse issues: education, family, law, etc. This list is by no means exclusive; these are the ones of which we have some personal knowledge/familiarity. This listing does not constitute an endorsement of these groups, but simply offers them as sources of useful information/services. Most of the groups have newsletters to which one may subscribe; some require a nominal cost; many are free. By subscribing to their mailing list, an individual/church/group can become well-informed on many vital issues of interest to Christians. While many of the groups are listed under one category, they are often active in other arenas as well. The classifications below represent only broad characterizations.

PRO-FAMILY GROUPS

AMERICAN FAMILY ASSOCIATION (AFA); Donald E. Wildmon, 107 Parkgate, PO Drawer 2440, Tupelo, MS 38803, 601-844-5036. A Christian organization promoting the Biblical ethic of decency in American society with primary emphasis on TV and other media.

CONCERNED WOMEN FOR AMERICA (CWA); Beverly LaHaye, 370 L'Enfant Promenade S.W., Suite 800, Washington, D.C. 20024, 202-488-7000. CWA emphasizes prayer and action; they organize united, effective prayer chapters to pray for the nation and its leaders and also give specific and current information on the status of movements/bills/ laws that would weaken the American family.

EAGLE FORUM; Phyllis Schlafly, Box 618, Alton, IL 62002, 618-462-5415. A group very active in pro-family issues and in educational curriculum content. Their regular publications include "The Phyllis Schlafly Report" and "The Education Reporter." Their achievements prove that citizen volunteers can determine governmental policies in Congress and State Legislatures, elect candidates at every level, and articulate pro-family policies in the media.

CHRISTIAN COALITION; Pat Robertson, Box 1990, Chesapeake, VA 23320, 804-424-2630. Christian Coalition promotes Christian values through a network of state affiliates and county chapters. Christian Coalition monitors legislative initiatives, takes concerted action to further traditional Godly interests, and interacts with state and local officials. They also train and equip individuals to become involved and to run for local offices.

FOCUS ON THE FAMILY ; Dr. James Dobson,Colorado Springs, CO 80995, 719-531-3400. A ministry dedicated to strengthening the family by providing information and practical applications on issues from relationships with children to relationships between spouses. Information is provided on social and political issues which have potential impact on the family.

CITIZEN MAGAZINE; A Publication of Focus on the Family, Tom Hess, Editor, Focus on the Family, Colorado Springs, CO 80995, 719-531-3400. Encourages people to apply Christian moral principles to community, state and national issues. It features articles about people who have made significant progress on a community or national issue, i.e., "inspiration," and informs people about significant issues of national/state interest which justifies a letter to the appropriate politician.

FAMILY RESEARCH COUNCIL; Dr. Gary Bauer, A Division of Focus on the Family, 601 Pennsylvania Ave., N.W., Suite 901, Washington, D.C. 20004, 202-393-2100. An organization for education, social policy research, and lobbying.

LEGAL GROUPS

CHRISTIAN ADVOCATES SERVING EVANGELISM (CASE); Jay Sekulow, 1201 Clairmont Rd. Ste. 100, Decatur, GA 30030, 404-633-2444. A Christian legal group successfully involved in defense of First Amendment issues of the free exercise of religion and of the freedom of speech on topics/subjects related to religion and religious principles.

AMERICAN CENTER FOR LAW & JUSTICE (ACLJ); Norm Berman, 1000 Centerville Turnpike, Virginia Beach, VA 23463, 804-424-7777, Ext. 2811. A state-by-state network of attorneys willing to stand up for God and decency in the courtrooms. The ACLJ takes the initiative in confronting the humanists, leftists, and the infamous ACLU who have been systematically destroying America's religious and moral foundations.

THE RUTHERFORD INSTITUTE; PO Box 4782, Charlottesville, VA 22906-7482, 804-978-3888. A non-profit civil liberties organization founded to defend the rights of religious persons and educate the public on important issues of religious liberty and the sanctity of human life.

THE NATIONAL LEGAL FOUNDATION; PO Box 64845, Virginia Beach, VA 23464, 804-424-4242. A public interest law firm dedicated to the preservation of First Amendment rights, specifically freedom of religion, speech, assembly and the press. This objective is accomplished through litigation and education.

CONCERNED WOMEN FOR AMERICA (CWA); 370 L'Enfant Promenade S.W., Suite 800, Washington, D.C. 20024, 202-488-7000. CWA provides legal services on issues based on Biblical, traditional moral, and pro-family stands in areas from education to public housing.

CHRISTIAN LAW ASSOCIATION; PO Box 30, Conneaut, OH 44030-0030, 216-493-3933; 216-599-8900. A legal ministry of helps to Bible-believing churches and Christians.

PRO-LIFE GROUPS

NATIONAL RIGHT TO LIFE NEWS; 419 7th Street N.W., Suite 500, Washington, D.C. 20004. Embraces an absolute commitment to truth, accuracy, and fairness to hasten the day that legal protection is returned to every person, born and unborn. Published twice monthly.

AMERICANS UNITED FOR LIFE; 343 S. Dearborn, Suite 1804, Chicago, IL 60604, 312-786-9494. Educational and legal pro-life group concerned with protecting human life at all stages of development. Issues of concern include abortion and euthanasia.

ANTI-PORNOGRAPHY GROUPS

CITIZENS FOR COMMUNITY VALUES; 11175 Reading Rd., Lower Level, Cincinnati, OH 45241, 513-733-5775. A group dedicated to the elimination of pornography and obscenity through law. Has been extremely effective in helping major cities become completely obscenity free.

NATIONAL COALITION AGAINST PORNOGRAPHY (NCAP); 800 Compton Rd., Suite 9224, Cincinnati, OH 45231, 513-521-6227. Their focus is to eliminate illegal pornography in the form of obscenity, especially child pornography. They educate the public, law-enforcement, government and community leaders through research and case studies. They involve individuals in supporting good legislation regarding this issue.

CHILDREN'S LEGAL FOUNDATION (Formerly Citizens for Decency Through Law); 2845 E. Camelback, Suite 740, Phoenix, AZ 85016, 602-381-1322. They strive to protect the innocence of children from the harms of obscenity and pornography. They fight child pornography and attempt to prevent pornographic materials from getting into the hands of youth.

EDUCATIONAL GROUPS

NAT'L ASSOC. OF CHRISTIAN EDUCATORS/CITIZENS FOR EXCELLENCE IN EDUC. (NACE/CEE); Dr. Robert Simonds, Box 3200, Costa Mesa, CA 92628, 714-546-5931. A grassroots Christian ministry dedicated to enabling families to reform and reshape public school education at the local level and thereby restore academic excellence, Godly morals, and traditional American values to the classroom. Helps organize local chapters to work with the local school officials to better education for America's children.

CHRISTIAN EDUCATORS ASSOC. (CEA); Forrest Turpin, PO Box 50025, Pasadena, CA 91105, 818-798-1124. A networking organization whose primary objective is to support Christian educators and equip them with the tools they need to have an indelible influence on America's youth. CEA provides counseling and referral services for specific questions in areas such as curricula, schoolbook policy, and legal rights.

AMERICANS FOR EDUCATIONAL CHOICE ; 927 S. Walter Reed Drive, Suite 1, Arlington, VA 22204, 703-486-8311. A coalition of organizations and individuals dedicated to: (1) freedom of parental choice of schools—public or private—without the loss of tax benefits; (2) freedom from excessive governmental regulation and control of schools.

RELEASED TIME BIBLE CLASSES; Maury Walker, 7436 Midiron Dr., Fair Oaks, CA 95628, 916-967-3972. A non-denomination religious instruction program for public school children based on traditional religious values. By Supreme Court decisions, with written permission, a child can be released from school for up to one hour per week for religious instruction.

HISTORICAL GROUPS

WALLBUILDERS; David Barton, PO Box 397, Aledo, TX 76008, 817-441-6044. A ministry dedicated to the recovery of those portions of American history which have now been removed from contemporary texts. After obtaining original copies of textbooks and works of the Founders, the information is then republished in its original form and distributed.

PROVIDENCE FOUNDATION; Stephen McDowell, Mark Beliles, 442 Westfield Rd., Charlottesville, VA 22901, 804-978-4535. They train Christians to reform the world around them from a worldview that is thoroughly Biblical. They provide excellent historical information and textbooks on early American History and education with a strong Biblical emphasis.

THE FOUNDATION FOR AMERICAN CHRISTIAN EDUCATION; 2946 25th Ave., San Francisco, CA 94132. Dedicated to the recovery and restoration of true American historical information. This group is famous for it "Redbooks" (books filled with photocopies of original American documents showing how the principles of Christianity filled public education and government affairs) and for "The Principle Approach" (the use of the philosophy and method of education used in America's schools in our earlier years).

PLYMOUTH ROCK FOUNDATION; Jack Coffield, PO Box 577, Marlborough, NH 03455, 603-876-4685. 20 years Christian ministry with a focus on: (1) American Christian heritage—research and publishing; (2) Christian education; (3) Current affairs from a Biblical viewpoint.

AMERICAN CHRISTIAN HISTORY INSTITUTE; James B. Rose, PO Box 648, Palo Cedro, CA 96073, 916-547-3535.

PILGRIM INSTITUTE; Ruth Smith, 52549 Gumwood Rd., Granger, IN 46530, 210-277-1789.

OTHER GROUPS

FAMILY RESEARCH INSTITUTE; Dr. Paul Cameron, PO Box 2091, Washington, D.C. 20013, 703-690-8536. It is dedicated to examining contemporary society through the lens of traditional morality and believes that society is best served by applying traditional Christian views of sexuality in social functioning.

NATIONAL CITIZENS ACTION NETWORK; David Balsiger, PO Box 10459, Costa Mesa, CA 92627-0459, 714-850-0349. Promotes Christian involvement in the elective and legislative process and encourages elected leaders to support traditional family values, a strong national security, and our constitutional freedoms. Publishes *The Presidential Biblical Scoreboard, The Family Protection Scoreboard,* and *Candidates Biblical Scoreboard* which provide voting records of elected officials and the stands of many candidates.

TIM LAHAYE CAPITOL REPORT; Box 2700, Washington, D. C. 20013, 202-488-0700. A publication providing regular information on issues of concern to Christians with updates on bills and issues from Washington, D.C.

Appendix B
Recommended Reading List

Books with Noncensored Views of
America's Christian History

This list is by no means exhaustive—there are many additional books available which provide excellent foundations on American heritage and history; however these are the ones with which we are familiar and which we can *recommend*. It is simply a list of books we have found useful in reclaiming and reteaching American history and American heritage. **Some of the books are available through nationwide distributors *(indicated by an asterisk—*)*, others are available only from the group or organization which authored the book.** If the book is distributed nationally it should be available through most Christian bookstores; if the bookstore does not stock the book, it should be able to order it.

THE MYTH OF SEPARATION* by David Barton. An examination of the quotes of the Founding Fathers and of Supreme Court rulings from 1793 to 1952 which establish that Christian principles were to be the basis for the governing of this nation and its schools. For example, our first Chief Justice of The U.S. Supreme Court declared that it was the duty of the people of this nation to elect Christians for their rulers. In 1844, the U.S. Supreme Court ruled that schools must teach morality and must use the Bible and Christian principles in their teaching. The same time Congress which approved the First Amendment (which the Court now uses to remove religious principles from schools) also required that a territory could not become a state in the United States unless it taught religion and morality in its schools. The book shows what our roots were, when and how we left them, and what the results have been. Makes revealing and exciting reading.

THE BULLETPROOF GEORGE WASHINGTON: AN ACCOUNT OF GOD'S PROVIDENTIAL CARE* by David Barton. This is a reprint of the story of the 23 year-old George Washington and his role in a prominent battle in the French and Indian War. This account appeared in virtually all history books from 1800-1932, but is now omitted. The story shows God's direct intervention and miraculous protection in the life of Washington.

THE NEW ENGLAND PRIMER, reprinted by David Barton. The *Primer* was first introduced into American schools in 1690 and was *the* textbook of American schools for over 200 years. Virtually every student learned to read from this book, as well as from the Bible. This is the same book from which the Founders learned valuable lessons about life's priorities. This is a reprint of the 1777 edition of *The New England Primer* and, with the tremendous lessons it provides, is profitable for all ages. May be ordered from WallBuilders, PO Box 397, Aledo, TX, 76008, 817-441-6044.

THE LIGHT AND THE GLORY* by Peter Marshall and David Manuel. This is a study of American history from the discovery of the nation under Columbus through the time of the Revolution.   Quoting from the book-jacket: "Did Columbus believe that God called him west to undiscovered lands? Does American democracy owe its inception to the handful of Pilgrims that settled at Plymouth? *The Light and the Glory* answers these questions, and many, many more. As we look at our nation's history from God's point of view, we begin to have an idea of how much we owe a very few—and how much is still at stake. *The Light and the Glory* reveals our true national heritage and inspires us to stay on God's course as a nation." *An **excellent** book!*

FROM SEA TO SHINING SEA* by Peter Marshall and David Manuel. This book is a continuation of the material presented in *The Light And The Glory*. It starts after the Revolution and goes through the Civil War, dealing with the westward expansion, the character of the pioneers, and slavery. It ends with the revivals that broke out following the civil war and their effects on society, revealing the grand purpose of America.

CHRISTIANITY AND THE CONSTITUTION* by John Eidsmoe. This book is an examination of the motives and intentions of the men who drafted the Constitution.   The findings are documented using the writings of the Founding   Fathers   themselves   and   accounts   written   by   their contemporaries.   The book deals with the political thinkers and social philosophies   that   influenced   the   Founders   including   Calvanism, freemasonry, Blackstone, Locke, and Montesquieu.   It also deals specifically with thirteen of the Founding Fathers and discusses the religious beliefs and practices of these men.   Also included is a discussion of the Constitution and the Biblical principles which are found in it.

THE MCGUFFEY READERS by William Holmes McGuffey.   Originally printed in 1836, the *McGuffey Readers* sold 122 million copies in their first 75 years. These *Readers*, the most widely used set in America's schools for decades after their introduction, contained a well-designed system of reading and provided excellent reading material for the students. McGuffey promoted desirable character traits in students through stories stressing honesty, integrity, industry and hard work, truthfulness, respect, kindness, etc. The stories he selected were a compilation of the best available stories for students. In the prefaces to his many works he openly indicated the primary source upon which he relied to teach these essential characteristics to youth: "From no source has the author drawn more copiously than from the Sacred Scriptures. For this certainly he apprehends no censure. In a Christian country, that man is to be pitied, who, at this day, can honestly object to imbuing the minds of youth with the language and spirit of the word of God." The reprinted McGuffey Readers may be ordered through the Moore Foundation, 36211 Sunset View, Washougal, WA, 98671, 206-835-5392 or 2736.

THE SOWER SERIES* by Mott Media. This is a series of books written about famous Christian individuals, holding forth their Christian character as a model for youth. Quoting from the book-cover: "Read for yourself... from the actual pen of these noted people from world history...of their relationship to Jesus Christ...and how that relationship affected their decisions...and the course of human history! See history come alive...learn of many hidden facts involving famous men and women from the pages of their diaries, letters to friends, books they wrote, etc...You'll be amazed at what has been left out of our history books!" The featured heroes include (there is a book about each hero): George Washington, Abraham Lincoln, Robert E. Lee, Abigail Adams, Christopher Columbus, Susanna Wesley, Clara Barton, Francis Scott Key, George Washington Carver, Isaac Newton, The Wright Brothers, and many others.

FAITH OF OUR FOUNDING FATHERS* by Tim Lahaye. Quoting from the book-jacket: "Were the men who carved this great nation out of the wilderness and drafted its founding documents God-fearing, Bible-believing Christians? Or, where they enlightenment Deists, Transcendentalists, and Unitarians?...What do the actual founding documents say? What do the intimate papers, diaries, and letters of the Founders themselves say?...This book solves the mystery of our nation's past. And...gives undeniable proof that those who established this country were, indeed, faithful Christians, or they were individuals who held firmly to a distinctively Christian view of what America—and the world—should be. This book is must reading for serious Christians. It will also become an excellent resource for use as a textbook in Christian schools everywhere."

AMERICA'S DATES WITH DESTINY* by Pat Robertson. Quoting from the book-jacket: "From the diary of America itself comes a view of history that has been virtually hidden from generations. The importance of God in the lives of our country's Founders and in the groundwork of this nation seems to have fallen through crevices of time, lost to those who have inherited a hard-fought democracy...Pat Robertson uncovers what the history books have altered and, in many instances, erased. The central role of Christian faith and biblical truth in shaping the charters of our original colonies, the curriculum of our original schools and universities, even the Declaration of Independence and the Constitution has been censored from the historic record...*America's Dates With Destiny* illuminates twenty-three extraordinary events in our nation's history, each date representing a crossroads in our democracy.   Through the spiritual directives of our forefathers...Robertson clearly shows us where we have been."

GOD AND GOVERNMENT: A BIBLICAL AND HISTORICAL STUDY* by Gary DeMar. This is a three-volume combination of textbook/workbook designed for individual, group, church, school, and seminar study. Quoting from the Foreword: "The Bible tells us that where there is no vision there is little, if any, future. A necessary ingredient in establishing a vision is the recognition of historical roots. To Americans this means a return to the Biblical foundation that undergirded early America and that has given form and content to our freedoms...Gary DeMar's study is important for the simple fact that he calls us back to our historical and biblical moorings—moorings that are essential for future liberty...He begins with the question: 'What does the Bible say about God and government?' From there, he analyzes the entire historical and governmental process according to the teachings of the Bible...Americans must again study the nature of their civil government. They must know why our society remains today the freest on the earth."

AMERICA'S PROVIDENTIAL HISTORY by Mark A. Beliles and Stephen K. McDowell. The book is a unique study of history, geography, economics, and government in the light of Biblical truths, providing concrete means for application of the truths studied. Quoting from Chapter 1: "The goal of *America's Providential History* is to equip Christians to be able to introduce Biblical principles into the public affairs of America, and every nation in the world, and in so doing bring Godly change through the world." May be ordered from The Providence Foundation, 442 Westfield Rd., Charlottesville, VA 22901, 804-978-4535.

Appendix C

1988 National Merit Program
Semi-Finalists

City , State	Total #	Public	%	Private	%
Birmingham, AL	28	14	50.0	14	50.0
Montgomery, AL	24	7	29.0	17	71.0
Phoenix, AZ	37	25	67.6	12	32.4
Tucson, AZ	41	33	80.5	8	19.5
Little Rock, AR	38	27	71.1	11	28.9
Los Angeles, CA	59	28	47.5	31	52.5
Mountain View, CA	7	3	42.9	4	57.1
Oakland, CA	32	7	21.9	25	78.1
Palo Alto, CA	54	46	85.2	8	14.8
San Diego, CA	69	62	89.9	7	10.1
San Francisco, CA	55	29	52.7	26	47.3
Wilmington, DE	22	10	45.5	12	54.5
District of Columbia	72	3	4.2	69	95.8
Ft. Lauderdale, FL	28	11	39.3	17	60.7
Jacksonville, FL	41	28	68.3	13	31.7
Miami, FL	57	38	66.7	19	33.3
Tampa, FL	52	25	48.1	27	51.9
Winter Park, FL	26	22	84.6	4	15.4
Atlanta, GA	80	38	47.5	42	52.5
Savannah, GA	11	3	27.3	8	72.7
Chicago, IL	77	27	35.1	50	64.9
Ft. Wayne, IN	28	17	60.7	11	39.3
Goshen, IN	5	1	20.0	4	80.0
Indianapolis, IN	50	38	76.0	12	24.0
South Bend, IN	26	18	69.2	8	30.8
Lexington, KY	37	29	78.4	8	21.6
Louisville, KY	76	43	56.6	33	43.4
Baton Rouge, LA	46	33	71.7	13	28.3
New Orleans, LA	93	41	44.1	52	55.9
Shreveport, LA	20	19	95.0	1	5.0
Baltimore, MD	35	15	42.9	20	57.1
Bethesda, MD	81	52	64.2	29	35.8
Andover, MA	35	5	14.3	30	85.7
Boston, MA	21	13	61.9	8	38.1
Concord, MA	14	6	42.9	8	57.1
Danvers, MA	15	0	0.0	15	100.0

City , State	Total #	Public	%	Private	%
Lexington, MA	18	18	100.0	0	0.0
Milton, MA	30	2	6.7	28	93.3
Ann Arbor, MI	58	45	77.6	13	22.4
Birmingham, MI	35	14	40.0	21	60.0
Bloomfield Hills, MI	29	11	37.9	18	62.1
Detroit, MI	12	5	41.7	7	58.3
Farmington Hills, MI	17	10	58.8	7	41.2
Flint, MI	8	6	75.0	2	25.0
Grand Rapids, MI	33	25	75.8	8	24.2
Kalamazoo, MI	14	11	78.6	3	21.4
Redford, MI	10	2	20.0	8	80.0
Minneapolis, MN	31	18	58.1	13	41.9
Rochester, MN	26	21	80.8	5	19.2
Jackson, MS	33	8	24.2	25	75.8
Natchez, MS	8	4	50.0	4	50.0
Kansas City, MO	24	8	33.3	16	66.7
Springfield, MO	22	20	90.9	2	9.1
St. Louis, MO	91	8	8.8	83	91.2
Billings, MT	16	16	100.0	0	0.0
Missoula, MT	9	8	88.9	1	11.1
Lincoln, NE	23	19	82.6	4	17.4
Omaha, NE	36	29	80.6	7	19.4
Concord, NH	21	4	19.0	17	81.0
Exeter, NH	36	0	0.0	36	100.0
Princeton, NJ	27	17	63.0	10	37.0
Albuquerque, NM	60	33	55.0	27	45.0
Bronx, NY	57	27	47.4	30	52.6
Brooklyn, NY	31	7	22.6	24	77.4
Buffalo, NY	18	8	44.4	10	55.6
New York, NY	213	138	64.8	75	35.2
Rochester, NY	41	30	73.2	11	26.8
Syracuse, NY	10	9	90.0	1	10.0
Asheville, NC	15	12	80.0	3	20.0
Charlotte, NC	48	35	72.9	13	27.1
Durham, NC	109	101	92.7	8	7.3
Greensboro, NC	21	19	90.5	2	9.5
Raleigh, NC	48	41	85.4	7	14.6
Winston-Salem, NC	28	22	78.6	6	21.4
Akron, OH	17	11	64.7	6	35.3
Cincinnati, OH	120	57	47.5	63	52.5
Cleveland, OH	19	5	26.3	14	73.7
Columbus, OH	37	24	64.9	13	35.1

City , State	Total #	Public	%	Private	%
Toledo, OH	40	11	27.5	29	72.5
Oklahoma City, OK	31	26	83.9	5	16.1
Tulsa, OK	53	29	54.7	24	45.3
Beaverton, OR	18	18	100.0	0	0.0
Portland, OR	35	25	71.4	10	28.6
Bethlehem, PA	13	8	61.5	5	38.5
Erie, PA	8	5	62.5	3	37.5
Lancaster, PA	10	8	80.0	2	20.0
Philadelphia, PA	61	21	34.4	40	65.6
Pittsburgh, PA	78	59	75.6	19	24.4
Providence, RI	22	9	40.9	13	59.1
Columbia, SC	44	42	95.5	2	4.5
Greenville, SC	12	6	50.0	6	50.0
Spartanburg, SC	23	18	78.3	5	21.7
Sioux Falls, SD	13	10	76.9	3	23.1
Chatanooga, TN	19	3	15.8	16	84.2
Knoxville, TN	32	22	68.8	10	31.2
Memphis, TN	63	27	42.9	36	57.1
Nashville, TN	36	14	38.9	22	61.1
Austin, TX	73	67	91.8	6	8.2
Dallas, TX	72	32	44.4	40	55.6
Ft. Worth, TX	29	17	58.6	12	41.4
Houston, TX	157	122	77.7	35	22.3
San Antonio, TX	80	72	90.0	8	10.0
Ogden, UT	2	2	100.0	0	0.0
Provo, UT	18	14	77.8	4	22.2
Salt Lake City, UT	41	39	95.1	2	4.9
Alexandria, VA	46	41	89.1	5	10.9
Arlington, VA	20	18	90.0	2	10.0
Fairfax, VA	35	32	91.4	3	8.6
Richmond, VA	20	13	65.0	7	35.0
Virginia Beach, VA	14	13	92.9	1	7.1
Bellvue, WA	15	13	86.7	2	13.3
Seattle, WA	87	59	67.8	28	32.2
Spokane, WA	24	19	79.2	5	20.8
Tacoma, WA	16	10	62.5	6	37.5
Charleston, WV	16	14	87.5	2	12.5
Parkersburg, WV	19	16	84.2	3	15.8
Madison, WI	37	35	94.6	2	5.4
Milwaukee, WI	36	13	36.1	23	63.9
Totals	4519	2746	60.8	1773	39.2

Footnotes

Preface

1. *Wallace v. Jaffree*, 105 F. 2d 1526, 1534 (11th Cir. 1983); *Wallace v. Jaffree*, 472 U.S. 37, 44 n. 22; *Jager v. Douglas*, 862 F. 2d 824 (11th Cir. 1989), *cert. denied*, 490 U.S. 1090; *Lundberg v. West Monona Community School District*, 731 F. Supp. 331, 342 (N.D. Iowa 1989); *Graham v. Central Community School District of Decatur County*, 608 F. Supp. 531, 535 (D.C. Iowa 1985); *Walter v. West Virginia Bd. of Educ.*, 610 F. Supp. 1169, 1176 n. 5 (D.C.W.Va. 1985); *Duffy v. Las Cruces Public Schools*, 557 F. Supp. 1013, 1019 (D.C.N.M. 1983); *United Christian Scientists v. Christian Science Board of Directors, First Church of Christ, Scientist*, 829 F. 2d 1152, 1166 (D.C. Cir. 1987); *Karen B. v. Treen*, 653 F. 2d 897, 901 (5th Cir. 1981), 455 U.S. 913, *affirmed; Weisman v. Lee*, 908 F. 2d 1090, 1097 (1st Cir. 1990); plus others.

Introduction

1. *Compton's Pictured Encyclopedia and Fact Index* (Chicago: F. E. Compton & Company, 1954), "The Story of Christianity," Vol. 3, p. 301.

2. Gary DeMar, *God and Government* (Atlanta: American Vision Press, 1982), p. 123. Quoting from John W. Whitehead, *The Separation Illusion: A Lawyer Examines the First Amendment* (Milford, MI: Mott Media, 1977), p. 18.

3. Noah Webster, *The History of the United States* (New Haven: Durrie & Peck, 1833), p. 309, ¶ 53.

4. James Madison, *Notes of Debates in the Federal Convention of 1787* (New York: W. W. Norton & Co., Original: 1787; reprinted 1987), pp. 209-210 (emphasis added).

5. Stephen K. McDowell and Mark A. Beliles, *The Spirit of the Constitution* (Charlottesville, VA: Providence Press, 1988).

6. Peter Marshall and David Manuel, *The Light and the Glory* (New Jersey: Fleming H. Revell Co., 1977), p. 343.

7. James D. Richardson, *A Compilation of the Messages and Papers of the Presidents, 1789-1897* (Published by Authority of Congress, 1899), Vol. 1, pp. 52-53.

8. *Id.* at 220 (emphasis added).

Chapter 1: 1962—A New Direction For America

1. *Engel v. Vitale*, 370 U.S. 421, 425 (1962).

2. *School Dist. of Abington Twp. v. Schempp*, 374 U.S. 203, 209 (1963).

3. *Stone v. Gramm*, 449 U.S. 39, 42 (1980).

4. *Graham v. Central Community School District of Decatur County*, 608 F. Supp. 531, 536 (W.D.N.Y. 1985).

5. *Kay by Disselbrett v. Douglas School District;* 719 F. 2d 875 (Or. Ct. App. 1986).

6. *Jager v. Douglas,* 862 F. 2d 824, 825 (11th Cir. 1989).

7. *State of Ohio v. Whisner,* 351 N.E. 2d 750 (Ohio Sup. Ct. 1976).

8. *Walz v. Tax Commission,* 397 U.S. 664, 702 (1970) (emphasis added).

9. *School Dist. of Abington Twp. v. Schempp,* 374 U.S. 203, 220-221 (1963) (emphasis added).

10. Lawrence A. Cremin, *1963 Yearbook,* World Book Encyclopedia, p. 38 (emphasis added).

11. Richard L. Worsnop, "Supreme Court: Legal Storm Center," *Editorial Research Reports,* Sept. 28, 1966, pp. 707-708 (emphasis added).

12. *Zorach v. Clauson,* 343 U.S. 306, 312 (1952).

13. *Collins v. Chandler Unified School District,* 644 F. 2d 759, 760 (9th Cir. 1981), *cert. denied,* 454 U.S. 863; *Stein v. Oshinsky,* 348 F. 2d 999 (2nd Cir. 1965), *cert. denied,* 382 U.S. 957.

14. *Reed v. Van Hoven,* 237 F. Supp. 48 (W.D. Mich. 1965).

15. *State of Ohio v. Whisner,* 351 N.E. 2d 750 (Ohio Sup. Ct. 1976).

16. John Eidsmoe, *Christianity and the Constitution* (Grand Rapids, MI: Baker Book House, 1987), p. 406.

17. William J. Murray, "America Without God," *The New American,* June 20, 1988, p. 19.

18. *Id.*

19. "Parent Silences Teaching of Carols," *Washington Times,* Dec. 12, 1988.

20. Stephen K. McDowell and Mark A. Beliles, *America's Providential History* (Charlottesville, VA: Providence Press, 1988), p. 79.

21. *City of Charleston v. S. A. Benjamin,* 2 Strob. 508, 520, 523 (S.C. Sup. Ct. 1846).

22. *People v. Ruggles,* 8 Johns 470, 545-546 (N.Y. Sup. Ct. 1811).

23. *Wallace v. Jaffree,* 105 F. 2d 1526, 1534 (11th Cir. 1983); *Wallace v. Jaffree,* 472 U.S. 37, 44 n. 22; *Jager v. Douglas,* 862 F. 2d 824 (11th Cir. 1989), *cert. denied,* 490 U.S. 1090; *Lundberg v. West Monona Community School District,* 731 F. Supp. 331, 342 (N.D. Iowa 1989); *Gramm v. Central Community School District of Decatur County,* 608 F. Supp. 531, 535 (D.C. Iowa 1985); *Walter v. West Virginia Bd. of Educ.,* 610 F. Supp. 1169, 1176 n. 5 (D.C.W.Va. 1985); *Duffy v. Las Cruces Public Schools,* 557 F. Supp. 1013, 1019 (D.C.N.M 1983); *United Christian Scientists v. Christian Science Board of Directors, First Church of Christ, Scientist,* 829 F. 2d 1152, 1166 (D.C. Cir. 1987); *Karen B. v. Treen,* 653 F. 2d 897, 901 (5th Cir. 1981), 455 U.S. 913, *affirmed; Weisman v. Lee,* 908 F. 2d 1090, 1097 (1st Cir. 1990); plus others.

24. *Engel v. Vitale,* 370 U.S. 421, 422 (1962).

Chapter 2: "Us"—The Youth

1. James D. Richardson, *A Compilation of the Messages and Papers of the Presidents, 1789-1897* (Published by Authority of Congress, 1899), Vol. 1, p. 220.

2. *Kendrick v. Bowen*, 657 F. Supp. 1547, 1562, 1563, 1564, 1565 (D.D.C. 1987)

3. Hon. Bill Bradley of the 76th State District of California prepared an informational packet excerpting books recommended by Planned Parenthood; information packet released by Bradley's office on January 15, 1987.

4. Wardell B. Pomeroy, Ph.D., *Boys and Sex* (NY: Delacorte Press, 1981).

5. Wardell B. Pomeroy, Ph.D., *Girls and Sex* (NY: Delacorte Press, 1981).

6. Rocky Mountain Planned Parenthood, *You've Changed the Combination* (Denver: RAJ Publications, 1977).

7. Pointed Publications, *The Great Orgasm Robbery* (Lakewood, CO: RAJ Publications, 1981), p. 15.

8. Alan Guttmacher Institute, "Teenage Pregnancy in Developed Countries," Volume 17, Number 2, March/April 1985.

9. Susan McBee, "A Call to Tame the Genie of Teen Sex," *U. S. News & World Report*, December 22, 1986, p. 8.

10. Interview with Josh McDowell over material in his book *Why Wait?* (San Bernadino, CA: Here's Life Publishers, 1987).

11. National Center for Health Statistics, "Advance Report of Final Natality Statitics, 1985," *Monthly Vital Statistics Report*, Vol. 36, No. 4, Supplement, July 17, 1987, U.S. Department of Health and Human Resources.

12. *Dallas Times Herald*, July 15, 1988, B-3.

13. Based on information provided by the Community Services Department of the Houston Independent School District in an interview on May 16, 1991.

14. Martha R. Burt, "Estimating the Public Costs of Teenage Childbearing," *Family Planning Perspectives*, Vol. 18, No. 5, Sept/Oct 1986. Supplied by Alan Guttmacher Institute.

15. Congressional Budget Office, Congress of the United States, *Sources of Support For Adolescent Mothers, September 1990*, p. 36. The study *Teenage Sexual and Reproductive Behavior in the United States*, published by the Alan Guttmacher Institute, 1991, reported the amount as $21 billion.

16. Lindsay van Gelder and Pam Brandt, "Teenage Pregnancy: The Crisis in America," *McCalls*, May 1987, p. 83.

17. *Id.*

18. *Time*, December 9, 1985, p. 79.

19. *Parade Magazine*, December 18, 1988. See also Hellmich, "Teens Having Sex by 16," *USA Today*, Sept. 22-24, 1989, p. 1A.

20. *Id.* at 3.

21. U.S. Department of Education review of the 1986 *Planned Parenthood Poll by Louis Harris and Associates, Inc.*, published on December 1, 1987, p. 2.

22. Study by the Rhode Island Rape Crisis Center released through the *Providence Journal-Bulletin*, May 1, 1988 (emphasis added).

23. *Id.*

24. Noah Webster, *The History of the United States* (New Haven: Durrie & Peck, 1833), p. 309, ¶ 53.

25. *Supra* note 1.

26. Percentages calculated from raw data obtained from Department of Health and Human Services and the Center for Disease Control.

27. Interview with Josh McDowell over material in his book, *Why Wait?* (San Bernadino, CA: Here's Life Publishers, 1987).

28. Percentages calculated from raw data obtained from Department of Health and Human Services and the Center for Disease Control.

29. *Family Planning Perspecitves*, "Teenage Pregnancy in Developed Countries," Vol. 17, No. 2, March-April 1985, Alan Guttmacher Institute. See also Robert Crooks and Karla Baur, *Our Sexuality* (Menlo Park, CA: The Benjamin/ Cummings Publishing Co., 1987), p. 443.

30. Robert Crooks and Karla Baur, *Our Sexuality* (Menlo Park, CA.: The Benjamin/Cummings Publishing Co., 1987), p. 441. See also Susan McBee, "A Call to Tame the Genie of Teen Sex," *U.S. News & World Report*, December 22, 1986, p. 8.

Chapter 3: "Our Parents"—The Family

1. *Grigsby v. Reib*, 153 S.W. 1124, 1129-30 (Tex. Sup. Ct. 1913).

2. *Sheffield v. Sheffield*, 3 Tex. 79, 85-86 (Tex. Sup. Ct. 1848).

3. James D. Richardson, *A Compilation of the Messages and Papers of the Presidents, 1789-1897* (Published by Authority of Congress, 1899), Vol. 1, p. 221.

4. "Runaway Youth: A Profile," *Children Today*, Jan/Feb 1986, p 4.

5. *Id.*

6. "Services to Runaways..." *Children Today*, Jan/Feb 1984, pp. 22-23.

7. *Id.*

8. "Adolescence: No Place Like Home," *Psychology Today*, December 1986, p. 12.

9. "Throwaways," *Ladies Home Journal*, January 1986, p. 44.

10. Glenn Collins, "Study Finds That Abuse Causes Children to Flee," *New York Times*, February 10, 1986.

11. *Id.*

12. *Id.*

13. *Id.*

14. Peter Schneider, "Lost Innocents: The Myth of Missing Children," *Harper*, February 1986, p. 50.

15. *Supra* note 3.

Chapter 4: "Our Teachers"—American Education

1. *Engel v. Vitale*, 370 U.S. 421, 425 (1962).

2. *Jager v. Douglas*, 862 F. 2d 824, 825 (11th Cir. 1989)

3. *School Dist. of Abington Twp. v. Schempp*, 374 U.S. 203, 209 (1963).

4. *Roberts v. Madigan*, 702 F. Supp. 1505, 1507 (D. Colo. 1989)

5. *Stone v. Gramm*, 449 U.S. 39, 42 (1980).

6. *Wallace v. Jaffree*, 472 U.S. 38, 57, 61 (1984).

7. *State of Ohio v. Whisner*, 351 N.E. 2d 750 (Ohio Sup. Ct. 1976).

8. National Commission on Excellence in Education, *A Nation at Risk: The Imperative For Educational Reform* (Washington, D.C.: U.S. Government Printing Office, 1983), p. 9.

9. "American Education: The ABC's of Failure," *Dallas Times Herald,* Dec. 11-21, 1983.

10. *Supra* note 8 at 23.

11. While overall retention rates have been improving, some segments of society (e.g., the Hispanic community) are experiencing a dropout rate as high as 40 percent. See U.S. Department of Education, *The Condition of Education, 1990* (Washington, D.C.: U.S. Government Printing Office), p. 22.

12. *USA Today,* Sept. 1985. See also *Christian School Comment,* Vol. 19, No. 3.

13. *Id.*

14. Information obtained from a joint-study by the National School Safety Center and the Virginia Department of Education.

15. Percentages calculated from published and unpublished statistical data from National Center for Health Statistics and Division of Vital Statistics of the Department of Health and Human Services.

16. Herbert Kohl, "What Teen Suicide Means," *Nation,* May 9, 1987, p. 603. See also *Newsweek,* March 23, 1987, pp. 28-29.

17. Suicide ranking information obtained from the National Center for Health Statistics, Statistical Resources Branch of the Division of Vital Statistics under the Department of Health and Human Services.

18. *Supra* note 8 at 8 (emphasis added).

19. Phyllis Schlafly, *Child Abuse in the Classroom* (Alton, IL: Marquette Press, 1984), p. 400 (emphasis added).

20. William J. Bennett—Secretary of Education, *American Education— Making It Work* (Washington, D.C.: U.S. Government Printing Office, 1988), p. 13 (emphasis added).

21. National Center for Educational Statistics—Department of Education, *The Condition of Education, 1987* (Washington, D.C.: U.S. Government Printing Office, 1987) p. 145 (emphasis added).

22. National Center for Educational Statistics—Department of Education, *The Condition of Education, 1990* (Washington, D.C.: U.S. Government Printing Office, 1990), pp. 7-8 (emphasis added).

23. *Wall Street Journal,* September 28, 1987.

24. *New York Times,* September 3, 1986.

25. Edwin West, *American Education,* Jan/Feb 1984.

26. James Madison, *Notes of Debates in the Federal Convention of 1787* (New York: W. W. Norton & Co., Original: 1787; reprinted 1987), pp. 209-210 (emphasis added).

Chapter 5: "Our Country"—The Nation

1. *Updegraph v. The Commonwealth*, 11 Serg. & R. 393, 402, 403, 406 (Pa. Sup. Ct. 1824).

2. *City of Charleston v. S. A. Benjamin*, 2 Strob. 508, 518, 523 (S.C. Sup. Ct. 1846).

3. *People v. Ruggles*, 8 Johns 545, 546 (N.Y. Sup. Ct. 1811).

4. Tim LaHaye, *Faith of Our Founding Fathers* (Brentwood, TN: Wolgemuth & Hyatt, 1987), p. 15.

5. This information is collected by Cambell University Law School and the Christian Legal Society and is documented in the monthly *Religious Freedom Reporter*.

6. James D. Richardson, *A Compilation of the Messages and Papers of the Presidents, 1789-1897* (Published by Authority of Congress, 1899), Vol. 1, p. 220.

7. Noah Webster, *The History of the United States* (New Haven: Durrie & Peck, 1833), p. 309, ¶ 53 (emphasis added).

8. *Supra* note 6.

9. "Thinking About Crime," by Edwin Meese III, *Harper's*, November 1985, Letters to the Editor.

10. Dorothy Scheuer, "What Crime Costs," *Scholastic Update*, September 30, 1983, pp. 5-6.

11. *Id.*

12. *Id.*

13. *Id.*

14. William Linn, *The Life of Jefferson* (Ithaca: Mack & Andrus, 1834), p. 265.

15. John Adams, *Works of John Adams, 2nd President of the United States*, collected by Charles Francis Adams, 1854.

16. Russ Walton, *Biblical Principles of Importance to Godly Christians* (New Hampshire: Plymouth Rock Foundation, 1984), p. 361; Stephen K. McDowell and Mark A Beliles, *Principles for the Reformation of the Nations*, p. 102; McDowell and Beliles, *The Spirit of the Constitution;* and Stephen K. McDowell and Mark A. Beliles, *America's Providential History* (Charlottesville, VA: Providence Press, 1988), p. 221.

17. Daniel Webster, *Works of Webster* (Boston: Little, Brown & Co, 1853), Vol. II, p. 615.

18. Donato Alvarez and Brian Cooper, "Productivity trends in manufacturing in the U.S. and 11 other countries," *Monthly Labor Review*, Jan. 1984, Vol. 107, pp. 56-57, U.S. Labor Dept. Statistics Bureau.

19. Martin Neil Baily, "What Has Happened to Productivity Growth?" *Science*, Oct. 24, 1986, Vol. 234, p. 443. Information referenced from Department of Labor, Bureau of Labor Statistics, *Productivity Indexes for Selected Industries, 1979 Edition* (Washington, D.C.: U.S. Government Printing Office, 1979), p.2

20. *Supra* note 6.

21. *City of Charleston v. S. A. Benjamin*, 2 Strob. 508, 520, 523 (S.C. Sup. Ct. 1846).

22. See "Sex, with Care," by Lewis J. Lord with Jeannye Thornton, Joseph Carey, and the Domestic Bureaus, *U. S. News & World Report*, June 2, 1986, p. 53.

23. *Id.* at 54.

24. See Paul J. Wiesner, M.D., "Magnitude of the Problem of Sexually Transmitted Diseases in the United States," *Sexually Transmitted Diseases—1980 Status Report*, p. 22. Reprinted by the U.S. Department of Health and Human Services, Public Health Service.

25. See "A Nasty New Epidemic—Concern is growing over sexually transmitted diseases," by Jean Seligmann with George Raine in San Francisco, Vincent Coppola in Atlanta, Mary Hager in Washington, Mariana Gosnell in New York and bureau reports, *Newsweek*, Feb. 4, 1985, p. 73.

26. See "Genital Herpes Infection—1966-1984," U.S. Department of Health and Human Services Public Health Service, MMWR, June 20, 1986, Vol. 35, No. 24, pp. 402-404.

27. *Supra* note 25.

28. See "Trends in Molluscum Contagiosum in the United States, 1966-1983," by Thomas M. Becker, M.D., Joseph H. Blount, M.P.H., John Douglas, M.D., and Franklyn N. Judson, M.D., *Sexually Transmitted Diseases*, Apr/Jun 1986, Vol. 13, No. 2, pp. 88-92, U.S. Department of Health and Human Services, Public Health Service.

29. *Supra* note 24 at 23.

30. *Supra* note 25 at 72.

31. *Id.* at 73.

32. *Id.* at 72.

33. *Id.* at 73.

34. *Id.*

35. *Id.*

36. *Supra* note 24 at 21.

37. Federal Bureau of Investigation, U.S. Department of Justice, *Uniform Crime Reports: Crime in the United States, 1990* (Washington, D.C.: U.S. Government Printing Office, 1990).

38. Richard A. Hawley, "School Children and Drugs: The Fancy That Has Not Passed," *Phi Delta Kappan*, May 1987, p. K1.

39. *Id.*

40. Fred M. Hechinger, "Concern Over Schooling of Military Recruits," *New York Times*, July 8, 1986.

41. *Safe Schools Overview*, National School Safety Center.

42. *The Almanac of the Christian World, 1991-1992* (Wheaton, IL: Tyndale House Publishers, 1991), p. 479.

43. *Supra* note 6.

Chapter 6: The Emergence of New National Problems

1. "America on Drugs," *U. S. News & World Report*, July 28, 1986, p. 48.

2. *Safe Schools Overview*, National School Safety Center.

3. Richard A. Hawley, "School Children and Drugs: The Fancy That Has Not Passed," *Phi Delta Kappan*, May 1987, p. K1.

4. Fred M. Hechinger, "Concern Over Schooling of Military Recruits," *New York Times*, July 8, 1986.

5. *Supra* note 2.

6. *Id.*

7. "The Drug Sources Must be Stopped," University of Michigan Survey, *Reader's Digest*, August 1983, p. 138.

8. *Education Week*, June 13, 1985, p. 28.

9. *Id.*

10. *Id.*

11. Janice C. Simpson, "A Shallow Labor Pool Spurs Businesses to Act to Bolster Education," *Wall Street Journal*, September 28, 1987.

12. Texas Literacy Council, "Developing Human Capital," p. 2, 1991.

Chapter 7: National Accountability and Biblical Repercussions

1. James Madison, *Notes of Debates in the Federal Convention of 1787* (New York: W. W. Norton & Co., Original: 1787; reprinted 1987), p. 504.

2. *Id.* at pp. 209-210.

3. Thomas Jefferson, *Notes on the State of Virginia* (Baltimore, 1800), Query XVIII; George Bancroft, *The History of the United States* (Boston: Little, Brown, and Company, 1875), Vol. X, p. 357; *The Story of Our Country* (Philadelphia: World Bible House, 1897), p. 282; James Truslow Adams, *America's Tragedy* (New York: Charles Scribner's Sons, 1934), p. 35; Benjamin Quarles, *The Negro in the American Revolution* (Williamsburg: Institute of Early American History and Culture & The University of North Carolina Press, 1961), p. 187; plus numerous others.

4. *Abraham Lincoln's Stories and Speeches*, J. B. McClure, editor (Chicago: Rhodes & McClure Pub. Co., 1896), pp. 185-186; John Wesley Hill, *Abraham Lincoln—Man of God* (New York, G. P. Putnam's Sons, 1920), p. 330. Also cited in Peter Marshall and David Manuel, *The Light and the Glory* (New Jersey: Fleming H. Revell Co., 1977), p. 295, and *The Encyclopedia of Religious Quotations*, Frank S. Mead, ed., (Westwood NJ: Fleming H. Revell Company, 1965), p. 265.

5. *Statistical Abstracts of the United States, 1990* (Washington, D.C.: U. S. Government Printing Office, 1990), p. 532, Table 879.

6. *Supra* note 2.

7. James D. Richardson, *A Compilation of the Messages and Papers of the Presidents, 1789-1897* (Published by Authority of Congress, 1899), Vol. 1, p. 220.

Chapter 8: An Analysis of the Problem

1. Lawrence A. Cremin, *1963 Yearbook,* World Book Encyclopedia, p. 38.

2. *Church of the Holy Trinity v. U.S.,* 143 U.S. 457 at 469-470 (1892)

3. *The Constitutions of the All the United States According to the Latest Amendments* (Lexington: Thomas T. Skillman, 1817), p. 224.

4. *Id.* at pp. 27-28. Also cited by Edwin S. Gaustad, *Faith of Our Fathers* (San Francisco: Harper & Row, 1987), p. 161.

Chapter 9: What Can Be Done Now?

1. Stephen K. McDowell and Mark A. Beliles, *America's Providential History* (Charlottesville, VA: Providence Press, 1988), p. 62.

2. John Bartlett, *Familiar Quotations* (Boston: Little, Brown & Co., 1980), p. 374.

3. Steve C. Dawson, *God's Providence in America's History* (Rancho Cordova, CA: Steve C. Dawson, 1988), p. I-8.

4. John Jay, *The Correspondence and Public Papers of John Jay, 1794-1826,* Henry P. Johnston, editor (New York: Burt Franklin, 1890; reprinted 1970), Vol. IV, p. 393.

5. *Id.* at 365.

6. Verna M. Hall and Rosalie J. Slater, *The Bible and the Constitution of the United States of America* (San Francisco: The Foundation for American Christian Education, 1983), p. 29. Also cited in McDowell and Beliles, *America's Providential History,* p. 221-222.

7. Charles G. Finney, Revival Lectures (Old Tappan, NJ: Fleming Revell Co., reprinted 1970), Lecture XV, pp. 336-337.

8. M. L. Weems, *The Life of Washington* (Philadelphia: Joseph Allen, 1800), p. 5-9.

9. Alexis De Tocqueville, *The Republic of the United States of America* (New York: A. S. Barnes & Co., 1851), p. 331.

10. Robert S. Lichter and Stanley Rothman, Research Institute on International Change, Columbia University, "Media Elite and American Values," *Public Opinion,* Oct/Nov 1981.

11. *Id.*

12. *Supra* note 7.

13. Peter Marshall and David Manuel, *The Light and the Glory* (Westwood, NJ: Fleming H. Revell Co., 1977), p. 370, n. 10 (emphasis added).

NOTES

NOTES

NOTES

NOTES

Price List

WallBuilders, Inc.
P.O. Box 397
Aledo, TX 76008
(817) 441-6044

Prices subject to change without notice
Quantity and case-lot discounts available

	Price/Copy	Quantity	Total
Books & Publications			
America: To Pray or Not To Pray?	$6.95	_____	_____
A statistical look at what has happened when religious principles were separated from public affairs by the Supreme Court in 1962 and at what can be done to repair the damage to the nation.			
The Myth of Separation	$7.95	_____	_____
An examination of the writings of the Framers of the Constitution and of the Supreme Court's own records proving that the separation of church and state is a recent innovation in America having no precedent in American history or legal practice.			
The Bulletproof George Washington	$4.95	_____	_____
Until 1934, this account of God's miraculous protection of Washington in the French and Indian War and of his open gratitude for God's Divine intervention could be found in virtually all student textbooks.			
The New England Primer	$5.95	_____	_____
A reprint of the 1777 textbook used by the Founding Fathers. The *Primer* was the first textbook ever printed in America (Boston, 1690) and was used to teach reading and Bible lessons in schools for over 200 years.			
What Happened in Education?	$2.95	_____	_____
Statistical evidence that disproves several popular educational explanations for the decline in SAT scores.			
Did Television Cause the Changes in Youth Morality?	$2.95	_____	_____
An examination to determine if TV caused the declines in youth morality that began in 1963. The results are very enlightening not only as to what happened in television, but when it happened, and why?			
Cassette Tapes			
"America's Godly Heritage" (See video)	$4.95	_____	_____
"Education and the Founding Fathers" (See Video)	$4.95	_____	_____
"The Spirit of the American Revolution"	$4.95	_____	_____
A look at the Christian motivation of the Founders throughout the American Revolution.			
"The Laws of the Heavens"	$4.95	_____	_____
An explanation of the eight words in the Declaration of Independence on which the nation was birthed.			
"America: Lessons from Nehemiah"	$4.95	_____	_____
A look at the scriptural parallels between the			

rebuilding of Jerusalem in the book of Nehemiah and that of America today.

"The Founding Fathers" $4.95   ____   ____
Highlights accomplishments and notable quotes of prominent Founding Fathers which show their strong belief in Christian principles.

"Keys to Good Government" $4.95   ____   ____
The Founding Fathers formula for good government.

"8 Principles for Reformation" $4.95   ____   ____
Eight Biblical guidelines for restoring Christian principles to society and public affairs.

"The Myth of Separation" (See book) $4.95   ____   ____

"America: To Pray or Not To Pray" (See book) $4.95   ____   ____

Video Cassette (VHS)

America's Godly Heritage (60 min.) $19.95   ____   ____
This clearly sets forth the beliefs of many of the famous Founding Fathers concerning the proper role of Christian principles in education, government, and the public affairs of the nation.

Education and the Founding Fathers (60 min.) $19.95   ____   ____
A look at the Bible-based educational system which produced America's great heroes and what they said and did (in their writings, laws, and Court decisions) to ensure that America would always continue to have that same Christian system of education.

Foundations of American Government (18 min.) $9.95   ____   ____
Surveys the historical statements and records surrounding the original drafting of the First Amendment and what has happened statistically since the 1962 Court rejected the Founders' intent.

Tax (TX only, add 7.75%): _____

Shipping (see chart at left): _____

TOTAL: _____

Shipping and Handling

Under $5.00	$1.50	$25.01-$ 40.00	$5.95
$ 5.01-$15.00	$2.95	$40.01-$ 60.00	$6.95
$15.01-$25.00	$3.95	$60.01-$100.00	$9.95

Canada orders add $5 extra.

Send The Above Indicated Materials To:

Name_____Phone ( )_____

Address_____

City_____State_____Zip_____

"You see the distress that we are in ... come, let us build the walls that we may no longer be a reproach." Nehemiah 2:17.